Restoring Tongues of Fire

Rekindling Tongues

and

Setting the World Ablaze for Jesus

John Caldwell

Commendations

This book was easy to pick up and difficult to put down. Deeply personal, and thoroughly Biblical. I believe it is sheer grace that John has written this book in this season, "to stoke the fire" in the reader's spirit (his words) and he certainly achieved it in mine!

Brian Campbell, Lead Pastor at CLC Wolverhampton

This book is fresh and challenging to the believer looking to seek being filled with the presence of and power of the Holy Spirit to witness. Even if one might agree to disagree on how that looks.

Timothy Ross PhD in Biblical Studies

This book is an insightful book on the gift of tongues. The insights, the testimonies, and the exegetical delivery of this work are excellent. Every Christian believer should read this."

Joel Tenney, Evangelist

Dedication

To Laura, my Father's Gift. Were it not for the precious ministry of the Spirit, providence would not have merged our paths at the right time and I would not have heard the Spirit's voice: "Do you not know this woman is going to become your wife?" I love you.

Contents

ACKNOWLEDGMENTS

There are so many people who have supported and helped shape this manuscript. It would be impossible to name everyone. However, I must thank the National Leader of the Apostolic Church UK, Ivan Parker. Your early input to my initial draft chapters both helped to encourage me that this was a worthwhile project, and it helped sharpen up some of my terminology. Thank you for taking the time, and thank you also for kindly offering to write the foreword.

Thank you to Liz Dobson for proof-reading the manuscript in record time. The manuscript is much more polished because of your work – any remaining blemishes are entirely my fault.

Thank you also to those who read early copies of this manuscript – your responses ("wow!" and "phenomenal") encouraged me greatly.

Thank you also to the folks who make up my Facebook community. Your comments on my questions, and feedback on my extracts have been a huge help. I can't name you all, but I want to thank Ben Thorp for asking the tough questions and Sam Gordon for his eagle-like vision that can spot any error in any manuscript. Thanks for spotting rogue periods and spaces – no one, literally no one else, would have noticed that. Yet that is the kind of small detail that's important when publishing a book. Thank you.

Thank you also to a number of friends in the US, Joel Tenney, Darlene Trowbridge, and Timothy Ross, your input was deeply appreciated.

Thank you to Allana, Janice, Graham, and John for supplying your testimonies. The manuscript is richer for it. You illustrate the thesis: *praying in tongues can set us ablaze for Jesus!*

A huge "thank you" must be given to my loving wife Laura who patiently endured "another book". Thankfully she loves God, and recognises the wind of God when it blows. Finally, I want to thank the God the Holy Spirit,. You bring it all to life, you guide my writing, and you draw me to Jesus.

Foreword by Ivan Parker

Did you know that only a small percentage of those who consider themselves to be Pentecostal, actively speak in tongues or exercise the gifts of the Holy Spirit? Has the Pentecostal church of today lost something of its incredibly powerful spiritual heritage in no longer emphasising the absolute necessity of the Baptism of the Holy Spirit and the signs that follow?

John Caldwell writes: "My aim is to do my bit to stoke the fire in your spirit!" well, I'm delighted to say that "Restoring Tongues of Fire" does just that!

With personal stories, the testimony of many others, and a whirlwind tour of Church history, this book takes the reader on a challenging journey that both educates and provokes.

In a world completely changed by the Covid-19 pandemic, the missional opportunities have multiplied exponentially for the church. That might be a daunting challenge, but "Restoring Tongues of Fire" equips and empowers the reader to receive or revive the Father's gift for all believers, and does so exhaustively and with great clarity.

Thoroughly and passionately John Caldwell not only inspires the reader, but through careful analysis and his skilful guidance through the scriptures, John stokes the spirit of any serious Christian to seek earnestly the Holy Spirit with signs following, so that personal passion and missional efficacy might return to those who do!

Ivan Parker, National Leader and Chair of the Trustees of the Apostolic Church UK

Introduction

Speaking in tongues is by far one of the most controversial subjects within the Christian faith. There are those who are supportive of the practice and emphasise it to an obsessive degree, there are those who reject the practice and are equally obsessive in attacking it, there are those who are confused by it and avoid it, and there are those who have never heard of tongues, despite being church-attending believers. The premise of this book is that none of these approaches are biblical. Speaking in tongues is clearly mentioned and taught in the scriptures, it is a manifestation of the Holy Spirit, which has been given to strengthen both the believer and the church. To reject or attack tongues is to reject or attack a work of the Holy Spirit, to neglect tongues is to neglect the work of the Spirit of God and to remain ignorant of tongues is to remain ignorant of an important aspect of the Spirit's ministry. It is my conviction that tongues is available for today, and it is available for all believers, and it is a manifestation of the Holy Spirit which needs to be expressed in a biblical and God-glorifying way.

In the early twentieth century, and again later in the sixties and seventies, speaking in tongues was restored to a place of prominence within the church. However, fifty years on, even in charismatic and Pentecostal circles, the manifestation of tongues lies dormant, tucked away, and out of sight.

It could be argued that the church is living in the post-charismatic era. Only a minority of believers now hold to cessationism – the school of thought that claims tongues, along with other spiritual gifts, have passed away. Whilst this school of thought prevailed, particularly in reformed and evangelical circles, for hundreds of years, it is now only a minority of believers who could be regarded as being strictly cessationist. If current estimates are accurate, charismatics make up the fourth greatest stream in Christianity, alongside Protestantism and Catholicism and Orthodox churches.

In many ways the landscape has changed for the better. The spiritual gifts have gone from the domain of fringe revival movements and have now been received by mainstream Christianity. The charismatic renewal in the seventies helped spread the gifts of the Spirit and a fresh work of the Spirit throughout all denominations. The Spirit blew through theological and denominational boundaries and manifested God's power and glory in the most unlikely of contexts. Reserved Anglicans found themselves rolling around the altar on the floor, Roman Catholics discovered a fresh passion for the gospel of grace and a desire to witness, even staunch Presbyterians were pelted by the Spirit's power and they went from being *the frozen chosen* to *happy clappy* at a single touch of God's presence, Baptists were baptised by fire, and many Brethren people received a new touch of God's power as the fire of God fell across the divided church. However, whilst the charismatic renewal has helped the wider church embrace the previously neglected gifts of the Spirit, it is also the case that widespread acceptance has grown to become widespread indifference. Much like the church prior to Constantine was rejected and despised, yet a powerful force for God, and once Christianity became the mainstream and widely accepted belief system and the cutting edge was exchanged for complacency; in the same way, this is what has happened to the Pentecostal and Charismatic renewals. As Pentecost became popular, Pentecostals lost both their hunger and the power, and charismatics became as culturally nominal as the mainstream institutions they originally hoped to renew. In other words, the charismatic renewal did not transform the institutions, instead the institutions institutionalised the charismatic renewal.

Towards the end of 2010, a poll was taken across 10 different countries[1] in order to gain an overview of how widespread Pentecostal phenomena is. The poll was striking, it showed that, "at least a quarter of the world's 2 billion Christians are thought to be members of these lively, highly personal faiths, which emphasize such spiritually renewing "gifts of the Holy Spirit" as speaking in tongues, divine healing and prophesying." However, it also revealed that almost 50% Pentecostals never speak or pray in tongues.

For non-Pentecostals these statistics won't signal a cause for concern, but for Pentecostals and charismatics, these figures are concerning. Speaking in tongues is to Pentecostals what Mass is to Catholics, and what believer's baptism is to Baptists. If you separate tongues from Pentecost, you no longer have Pentecost. If Pentecostals have stopped praying in tongues, it needs to be asked, in what sense are they Pentecostal? The information revealing the

---

[1] The United States; Brazil, Chile and Guatemala in Latin America; Kenya, Nigeria and South Africa in Africa; and India, the Philippines and South Korea in Asia. Spirit and Power - A 10-Country Survey of Pentecostals | Pew Research Center (pewforum.org)

decline in tongues is not just the statistics of some stand-alone poll. Many seasoned preachers, pastors and authors have also noticed the trend. Charismatic leader, Bert Farias notes:

> I travel to churches for a living so I see first-hand how much of a diminishing emphasis there is on praying in tongues these days. There is a marked difference between now and just 20-30 years ago. Even in the back room in pre-service prayer there seems to be less and less of praying in tongues. And singing in tongues is even rarer and almost unheard of. More and more Christians seem to be uncomfortable and unfamiliar with this realm. This neglect is hurting the church. This de-emphasis is diminishing her power and effectiveness. And this is exactly what the devil wants.[2]

I don't mean to suggest that speaking in tongues is all there is to Pentecostal and charismatic identity. It's not. However, there is a correlation between praying in tongues and the other manifestations of the Spirit. Many of the Pentecostal forefathers considered the baptism in the Holy Spirit and speaking in tongues to be the gateway to other gifts of the Spirit. Farias, again, notes how the early Pentecostal pioneers recognised the connection between praying in tongues and other signs and wonders. Farias

---

[2] https://www.charismanews.com/opinion/the-flaming-herald/52064-why-do-so-many-pentecostals-and-charismatics-not-speak-in-tongues-anymore

says:

> Tongues was the making of such world changing ministries as John G. Lake, Oral Roberts, and Kenneth E. Hagin. Someone asked Lester Sumrall how often he prayed in tongues, which generated this terse respond: "When I'm not preaching."

Farias is making an incredible point. He is reminding us that the mighty miracles of healing and deliverance that God did through the early pioneers were inseparably linked to their lifestyle of praying in tongues. Why are Pentecostals and charismatics no longer seeing the miracles, the conversions and the revivals that marked their early movements? Many have forgotten the key to God's power and presence: praying in the Holy Spirit.

This is one of the reasons I am moved to write this book. Yes there are countless books already written on the subject of tongues. Yes there will be more scholarly, and more popular books than this one. But my aim is not to be popular nor is it to be scholarly. My aim is to do my bit to stoke the fire in your spirit! My aim is pastoral, perhaps even a little apostolic. We need the presence of God in our lives and in our churches more than ever before. A tide of darkness is sweeping the nations. The church, and many believers are weak. Yet God has given us a gift – a gift whereby we can edify ourselves "He who speaks in a tongue edifies himself."

1 Cor. 14:4. Praying tongues builds up our inner man. It strengthens our weary souls. It draws us up out of the pit and launches us into the heavenly places – our true resting place in Christ! Praying in tongues releases the explosive power of the Kingdom of God in us and through us. We neglect this gift to our own detriment!

Let us cast aside all indifference, or fear, or even hostility towards this gift and let us look to God and his word for his revelation on the subject. Throughout this book we are going open the pages of *the* Book and let God speak. When it comes to speaking in tongues, very often the truth is eclipsed by tradition. Let us lay aside all tradition and human reasonings and seek God for his truth on the matter and once we see it, let us press in and receive all that God has for us. The world is waiting for a fresh demonstration of God's power and glory. This is what followers of Jesus are called to, but we must be willing to pick up the blazing baton of the burning presence of God. Let us rekindle tongues and set the world ablaze for Jesus!

1 My Personal Experience

Before we get into the theology of tongues, and the exegesis of biblical texts, let me share with you my own experience and journey with the Holy Spirit and speaking in tongues. I was born again around January 1999. That experience changed my life. A love for God was birthed within my spirit. My life was now set on a completely new journey. A few months later I had series of experiences with God's presence. The first of these shook me to the core of my being. It was an encounter with the burning, Holy presence of God. The outcome of this experience was a deep consciousness of the fear of God.

The second of these experiences was less intense, but it was no less deep. I was led to a fresh place of surrender and consecration; I was filled with the Holy Spirit and I was set free from a 5 year nicotine and alcohol addiction.

It was shortly after this experience that I experienced tongues. In the early hours of the morning, I was lying awake in my bed, and praying. Suddenly new words that I did not understand seemed to rest on the tip of my tongue. I began to speak these words quietly and every time I did a wave of peace would flow over me. I was praying in tongues.

As a young Christian, I was unsure about tongues. My own church did not believe in tongues, but I'd also met a number of Pentecostal believers through the ministry of Teen Challenge. These believers were very passionate, and they were convinced that God was a God of miracles *today*. Whereas the network of churches where I had come to hear the gospel, trust in Christ, and get baptised by immersion as a believer, were cessationist. They taught that the gifts of the Spirit had passed away sometime after the death of the last apostle. As a new believer I had been encouraged not to seek the gifts of the Spirit. I was taught that Pentecostals were in error, and that tongues, prophecies, and miracles were no longer to be expected today.

There was a problem though. I had encountered the presence of the risen Christ. An experience of God was at the heart of my conversion, yet I found myself amongst a group of Christians who loved the Bible and loved God, but who were cautious and anxious about spiritual experiences and supernatural gifts.

Further, I had been taught by the leaders of this church that tongues were a Spirit empowered ability to speak *earthly languages* for *the purpose of evangelising* people from other cultures and languages. Wasn't this what Acts 2 revealed about tongues? After the Holy Spirit was poured out, the believers began to speak in tongues, and an international crowd gathers and then asks: "And how is it that we hear, each in our own language in which we were born?" (Acts 2:8 NKJ) How could I *know* what language I was speaking? How could I know it *was* a language? How can tongues as experienced today be an unintelligible language when what happened in Acts 2 involved *real* languages?

As I lay in bed praying in a new tongue, I felt led to turn to 1 Corinthians 14. I had read this passage a few times before, but I could never understand it. As I opened the Bible my eyes were drawn to the verse: "For he who speaks in a tongue does not speak to men but to God, for *no one understands him*; however, *in the spirit he speaks mysteries*." (1 Cor. 14:2 NKJ) The verse was plain as day. Tongues, as Paul is describing it here, is not a gift to speak a language that can be understood naturally. It is not an earthly language as such. If it were, Paul could not say "no one understands him" he would have to say: "only the person who speaks that language can understand." No, this was a language whereby I could communicate directly with God. My born-again spirit was praying. By praying in tongues, I was praying the mysteries of God in a language that could not be understood unless God gave the gift of interpretation.

It's not my purpose to expound these texts fully at this point. We will look at them in a later chapter. I'm just sharing what happened that night. Or rather in the early hours of the morning. This new language was accompanied by peace, which is a fruit of the Holy Spirit, and I was led to test the experience against the Word of God, and the Spirit then shed light on the scriptures. I was now persuaded that this was the work of God, I shut my Bible turned off my bedside lamp, and fell asleep praying in tongues and delighting in God.

There were also a few prophetic things that surrounded this experience. Earlier that evening (the Saturday night) I had attended a broadly charismatic gospel meeting in the town centre. During the meeting, one of the pastor's daughters brought a prophetic word. She said something like: "God has placed before you a banquet. There's a full feast spread out for you. He doesn't just want you to take a little bit here and reject the rest. He wants you to experience all that he has provided for you at this banqueting table." This came back to me at some point and I now realised that the prophecy was for me. I had been cautiously holding back from all that God had for me by not embracing the gifts that he was seeking to give me. God was now calling me to receive all that he had for me, and the first part of that journey involved speaking in tongues. I had no idea how much this gift would change my prayer life and launch me into other gifts of the Spirit.

The second prophetic circumstance was the date that this happened. It was Pentecost Sunday, the year 2000. The significance did not strike me at the time. It was only many years later that I realised that I had received this filling of the Spirit, and the ability to speak in tongues in the early hours of Pentecost Sunday. To me, that was the Father's providential way of saying to me that what I have received is the same as what the early disciples received two thousand years earlier. Two thousand years after Pentecost, on the very day of Pentecost, I received my own Pentecost.

These prophetic providences are important. One of the areas the devil attacks is the gifts of the Spirit. He hates them because they are the power tools of the church. The gifts of the Spirit are the church's weapons of mass destruction against the kingdom of darkness. It's important to remind ourselves of God's prophetic providences because the enemy will seek to cause us to doubt our experiences and neglect the gifts. The devil has aggressively attacked the gifts of the Spirit a few times in my Christian walk.

I will talk about these a little later, but first let me share some more about how the filling of the Spirit and tongues launched me into a new dimension in my walk with Christ.

When I was baptised as a believer by immersion, following my personal encounter with Christ, a Christian gave me a baptism card with the following verse: "The Spirit of the LORD will come powerfully upon you, and you will prophesy with them; and you will be changed into a different person." (1 Sam. 10:6 NIV) This was a promise from God to Saul as Samuel the prophet anointed him to become King. The point is this: The Holy Spirit was going to transform Saul, and he did.

Sadly, many evangelicals who love the Bible have a tendency to disconnect the work of the Spirit in Old Testament kings and prophets from the work of the Spirit today. The work of the Spirit under the New Covenant is even greater than the work of the Spirit under the Old Covenant. In the Old Covenant the Spirit only rested upon a few anointed individuals, under the New Covenant the Spirit dwells within and comes upon New Covenant believers. The effect should be the same – we should be changed into a different person.

Many people don't like that idea. Objections about our God-given personality immediately rise to the surface when we hear this. I can only share my experience – that verse was prophetic. It actually happened in my life. When the Spirit came upon me, and the gifts began to flow, I was changed into a different person. When I first came to Christ I was timid, broken, tongue-tied, unclear in my thinking, socially awkward and fearful. Those who only know me today will struggle to believe that. Yet it's true. But when the Holy Spirit came upon me, the following verse started to become a reality: "For God has not given us a spirit of fear, but of power and of love and of a sound mind." (2 Tim. 1:7 NKJ)

This does not mean the Holy Spirit takes over your personality, it means the Holy Spirit transforms your personality and your character. The Holy Spirit will heal the broken areas, draw out gifts and strengths, and he will enable you to overcome the weaknesses of your personality. Too many believers are resistant to this transforming work of the Holy Spirit. Fear keeps us bound. We would rather manage ourselves in the flesh than allow the Spirit to work on the inside. Too many of us prefer to use natural coping mechanisms rather than yielding to the inner working of the

Spirit. We believe lies like: "I'm just shy and reserved, I could never speak to anyone about my faith." That's just a lie of the devil, and it's also fleshly pride. It's disobedience towards the Lord who tells us, "in your hearts revere Christ as Lord. Always be prepared to give an answer to everyone who asks you to give the reason for the hope that you have. But do this with gentleness and respect." (1 Pet. 3:15 NIV)

One of the first changes that the Lord birthed within me through the ministry of the Holy Spirit and praying in tongues was a deep burden to reach the lost. I couldn't walk down the street without an overwhelming consciousness of the stream of people passing me by on their way to a lost eternity. The Lord led me to hand out tracts to people, to speak to homeless folk, to share my testimony with folks on the street who were clearly caught up in addiction.

The Lord led me into a season of reaching out to addicts and alcoholics – how could I not? The Lord had taken me out of that pit, how could I not help others find the way?

The baptism of the Holy Spirit, and speaking in tongues, has often been described as the gateway to the other gifts of the Holy Spirit. In experience, I can see that this is true. We can also see it in scripture. Stephen was led on journey from the receiving the gift of the Spirit, to being a man of faithfulness and encouragement, to being set apart to serve as a deacon, to a powerful ministry of gospel proclamation with signs and wonders. Stephen wasn't an apostle, but the Lord used him to carry out signs and wonders. The Holy Spirit had got a hold of Stephen.

For me, when I first got saved, and prior to the deepening work of the Spirit, I looked for opportunities to serve. I offered to help an older couple in the church with gardening. Later I started to volunteer at addiction outreaches. I started by making the tea, this led to conversations which then led to sharing about Jesus and praying for folk. Before long I was learning to pray for the sick, prophesy, and teach the Word of God to others. The gifts were flowing. This is scriptural. In the parable of the talents, we learn that when we use what God has given us in the right way, it multiplies. When we bury the gifts of God, we will lose even what we have. If we are truly born-again believers, the Spirit has been given to us, but if we don't open ourselves up to his fullness and working, we will not develop and multiply our gifts, and we will not experience the very basic benefits of the gift that we have been given.

One of the strongest gifts that has emerged in my own life, in recent years, is the gift of preaching. I often feel the fire of God when I stand in the pulpit and preach the Word. Others sense it too. This gift isn't natural. Some folk, who are not used to experiencing an anointing in church, will say to me, "You are really confident," or "You are very passionate." But that's not really true. What people are seeing is boldness, and that boldness comes from the Holy Spirit. It's not self-confidence – I never had anything to be self-confident about. I came to Christ with nothing. It's *confidence in Christ*. One of the hallmarks of the apostles after Pentecost was boldness: "Now when they saw the boldness of Peter and John, and perceived that they were uneducated, common men, they were astonished. And they recognized that they had been with Jesus." (Acts 4:13 ESV) These were the very same guys who were hiding away fearful of persecution prior to Pentecost. Likewise, the filling of the Spirit and speaking in tongues has sparked the same fire in my spirit. The Holy Spirit has taken me from a place of timidity to a place of boldness.

There is a cost. We need to be willing to crucify our so-called reputation. If we are more concerned about our appearance and how others perceive us, we will never experience the fullness of the Spirit. We need to be willing to be a fool for Christ. Some of us want to cling on to respectability whilst trying to reach the lost at the same time. It doesn't work that way. The message of the cross is always foolishness. It's not reasonable. We need to decide that we will speak *what* God tells us *when* he tells us without compromise, no matter the backlash. The great thing is that sometimes we will see powerful results but other times we will receive opposition. The results are not for us to worry about. We are called to be faithful.

Another major aspect that praying in tongues will help us develop is our ability to follow divine guidance. He will lead us into divine appointments if we are sensitive to his voice. We see this with Philip the evangelist. "Then the Spirit said to Philip, "Go near and overtake this chariot."" (Acts 8:29 NKJ) We are not told *how* the Spirit spoke to Philip, we are just told that the Spirit spoke to him and he obeyed. The outcome was incredible. A divine appointment. A soul was saved because of Philip's sensitivity to the Spirit and his obedience. This stuff is not reserved for the book of Acts, it's for all of us.

A friend and I were on our way on a mission trip to the Isle of Lewis. Before we left the mainland, we stopped at McDonald's. Whilst in the queue, a biker came in and I sensed the Lord tell me that he had been thinking of becoming a Christian. I also sensed the Lord tell me to go and ask him. I approached him and asked if him if he'd been thinking about becoming a Christian. He said he had been! I then had an opportunity to share the gospel with him and lead him to Christ in McDonald's. God is good! How many people are at that same point, and how many of us are sensitive to the Spirit's leadings? I have to confess, I don't always follow the still small voice, but I do desire to press into his leading much more.

There are many more stories I could write, I could talk about healings, significant prophetic words, encounters with demonic forces, and divine appointments – but space does not permit. However, I firmly believe that these experiences would not have happened had I not been filled with the Holy Spirit and received tongues. It was this experience that launched me into a Christianity that looks, sounds and feels like the book of Acts. It is no coincidence that those of us who neglect or reject this experience also fail to experience anything close to the kind of Christianity that we see in the book of Acts. God's purposes have not changed. The world still needs to be reached for Christ. Neither have his methods changed. He is still looking for a people who will simply receive the fullness of his Spirit and obey the Great Commission in his strength.

2 The Devil's Strategy: Neglecting the Gifts

The devil hates the ministry of the Holy Spirit. He will do what he can to sow doubt in the mind of believers concerning the Spirit's work. He will claim a work of God is a work of Satan so that believers will reject the Spirit's ministry.

As I was writing this section of the manuscript, I'd asked some friends to send me testimonies about how their experience with the Spirit and tongues had transformed their walk with God. We will see those later, but I want to share this one just now. It's about the devil's opposition to the ministry of the Holy Spirit in general, and tongues in particular. A pastor sent me this:

> I think the enemy can even strategize to knock out the gift as it is so powerful and as such is like a gateway to the other gifts. Sometimes I will speak in tongues and then can hear (from

God) clearly to give a word of knowledge or something prophetic. Back to the strategies of darkness: I was driving home today and haven't been using the gift much lately so started to stir myself up. I realized, very subtly, I had begun to believe that it wasn't that important (Wow! After the testimonies I have given about the power of tongues). I repented and then began to hear (from God) more clearly and the Spirit led me in a wholehearted "Holy! Holy! Holy is your name!" I find personally that the Spirit helps me worship in tongues and then I hear even better as I become filled with the Spirit (Another benefit!). Well on the way home driving, I am worshipping away in tongues and English, and I asked the Lord why I had subconsciously started believing it wasn't that important. I heard that I was helped along by strategies of darkness. Targeted witchcraft (There is a ton of that here). Anyway, I sense a real 'pick me up' in my spirit man since I had this time.

Many of us who have experienced the ministry of the Holy Spirit and the gifts of the Spirit will relate to this pastor's testimony. There are times when we may drift from the source of blessing. We need to understand that both our flesh and the enemy are resistant to the Spirit. The devil uses many strategies to cause us to neglect or reject the gifts. We may just think that we have matured, but the reality is we may have become proud and self-sufficient. Ironically, this is what happened to Saul – the very one who experienced the Spirit's transforming presence. Regarding Saul, "Samuel said, "Although you were once small in your own eyes, did you not become the head of the tribes of Israel? The LORD anointed you king over Israel." (1 Sam. 15:17 NIV) In other words, Saul had gone from being humble and God-dependent to becoming proud, presumptuous and self-sufficient. We often miss the point of these narratives. Many evangelicals divide bible characters into heroes and villains. They don't realise that these characters are pictures of ourselves. Saul is a lesson for every believer. We can all move from child-like faith to self-sufficiency – and the journey is as subtle as it is tragic. Many of us who once rejoiced in the freshness of the Spirit's gifts have grown cold. And the real tragedy is that just like Saul, we don't even know it's happened.

When I first came to Christ, an older believer encouraged me to always keep my testimony fresh in my mind because the devil will come and try to cause me to doubt my salvation. I've discovered this is also how he works with the ministry of the Holy Spirit. He will use fear to prevent a Christian receiving the fullness of the Spirit and his gifts, but if that Christian pushes through and receives the Holy Spirit's ministry, the devil will then come and try to get the

Christian off course.

This happened to me quite early on. At the turn of the millennium the internet was becoming a thing. Having just found a new dimension to my walk with Jesus, I began to use the internet to learn more about the gifts of the Spirit. Nightmare. Google "Spiritual Gifts" or "Pentecostalism" and bang! You are presented with a ton of information discrediting everything and anything relating to charismatic Christianity. You discover the extreme end of the movement, you discover heresy hunters and their warnings against the gifts of the Holy Spirit, you find videos of every foolish thing that has been done in the name of the Holy Spirit and you will be told that charismatic experience is a deception. No believer wants to be deceived, so this can cause younger Christians or new Christians to be anxious that they are being misled. As a young Christian, I was committed to the doctrine of scripture. The Bible is the Word of God, and I wasn't prepared to put experience above God's revelation. On the one hand, it was good to be made aware of the dangers, on the other hand this experience caused me to doubt the credibility of the wider charismatic movement – even the good parts.

For me, this led to the tension of what it means to be a "Word and Spirit" Christian. Although I didn't know the term at the time nor did I know there was a "Word and Spirit" movement. Neither did I know that there were countless books that could have helped me. I was yet to discover the works of Martyn Lloyd Jones, Terry Virgo, R.T. Kendall, J.I. Packer, John Piper, John Owen, Sam Storms, Gordon Fee, Keith Warrington and a host of others who were not only solid in their evangelical commitments, but also, to varying degrees, open to the supernatural work of the Holy Spirit. In the meantime, I plodded along in my faith devouring whatever books I happened to stumble upon.

Eventually my doubts about the Holy Spirit's ministry diminished and I just pressed on with the work of local mission. During that season I experienced a wonderful wave of the Holy Spirit during a time of youth ministry with Paisley YMCA. We saw many young people touched and impacted by the presence of God. Whilst YMCA was non-denominational, it was the combination of Christian staff, Spirit-filled believers, the local Elim church and Teen Challenge USA that helped to trigger this outpouring of the Spirit. Young people came to faith, they became evangelists, and they had supernatural encounters. God was moving.

Yet even after this powerful season of the Spirit's power, I have at times (like the pastor who shared his testimony above) drifted from a full-on pursuit of the presence and purpose of God. As I have talked to others over the years, I have learned that this is true for many. I recall one Baptist minister share with me that he received the baptism of the Holy Spirit and tongues through the ministry of Hugh Black, a late and well-loved Pentecostal pastor and evangelist. Yet, this same pastor confided that he hardly uses the gift now because he regards it as a gift for infancy, it is for those who lack theological language. Now that he had studied theology, he a had greater language that he could use to speak to God. My heart sank. I knew there was something wrong with that view. Yet, if I am honest, as the years have passed I also at times have allowed the gift to be shelved and I haven't drawn from it as much as I should or could have.

John Wimber is another example. Many people know John for the incredible focus he brought on the ministry of signs and wonders and mission. Yet not many know that John quenched the ministry of the Spirit for many years. He had operated in the gift of healing, but he then set the gifts aside and focused on church ministry without the gifts of the Spirit. I can relate to that too.

When we look at some of the chaos within charismatic Christianity, we have to confess that it is no surprise that some Christians want nothing to do with the gifts. There is a lot of chaos. There is a lot of error. We have to acknowledge that there is a valid reason for pastors like John MacArthur to hold conferences and write books about 'Strange Fire'. There is strange fire. A number of years ago I became persuaded that if we just focused on right doctrine, the gospel and church order, then that was all that mattered. What I eventually discovered is that without the Spirit's presence and power, we can't have church order – and our doctrine isn't as good as we think, and our gospel will lack the power it is designed to carry. We cannot separate the Word and Spirit. Yet this is the very thing the devil works hard to do. Abuse of the gifts of the Spirit should not lead to the neglect of the gifts, it should lead to correct use of the gifts! Just because there are heresies, sins, and scandals within the Pentecostal movements does not mean there is not a genuine work of the Holy Spirit. We must remember that the New Testament letters were written to churches that were full of schism, heresy, and sin. Yet Paul still addressed them as churches. We need to remember that no branch of the church has been free from scandal. Fallen leaders are found in every movement. In fact, the reason these things often happen is because the devil is aggressively attacking any genuine work of the Holy Spirit. He only counterfeits what is real. Just because there are deceptions does not mean there is not an authentic ministry of the Holy Spirit.

If the devil can cause us to reject or neglect the power of the Spirit, he is able to render us ineffective. When we move in the power of the Spirit we start to take territory for the Kingdom of God. The devil hates giving up territory. This work of taking territory must begin with us. If God does not take ground in our souls, we cannot take ground in the world. This is why praying in tongues is the gateway to a greater manifestation of the Kingdom of God. When we pray in the spirit we begin to take ground within our own souls. We begin to drive out discouragement, apathy, lust, anger, unbelief and a host of other enemies. Like Israel of old we are called to take the land and drive out everything that opposes God. Praying in tongues is a primary weapon that God gives us to press into the fullness of our inheritance. Once we have waged war and conquered our own souls, we can then start to wage war in other spheres.

The primary aim of this book is not to argue with or convince those who are opposed to the gifts. The primary aim is to stir up the gift in those who have let the fire die down to an ember. For some of us it even looks like the fire has totally died. However, if we start to stir up tongues, a fresh wind will start to blow over our souls. Those charcoaled coals will begin to glow again. As we press into God, our souls will be transformed from an ember to a flame and as we persevere in our prayer language the flame will become a fire! The world needs us to be burning with the fire of God. It's time to fan the flame!

For this reason I remind you to fan into flame the gift of God, which is in you through the laying on of my hands. (2 Tim. 1:6 NIV)

Some Christians are incredibly intellectual. Their Christianity is dominated by their mind. Others are more motivated by the heart. However, biblical Christianity is *both* head and heart. And we need to be aware that both our minds and our hearts can be influenced by the flesh. Both the mind and the heart must become subject to the Holy Spirit. Jesus commands us to: "Love the Lord your God with all your heart and with all your soul and with all your mind and with all your strength." (Mk. 12:30 NIV) Notice the three dimensions – heart, mind, and soul (or spirit). If you are a believer who has a strong mind, you may find it difficult to bring your heart and spirit into alignment with the Holy Spirit. Whilst you oppose tongues on intellectual grounds, the deeper issue may be that you have become self-sufficient in the area of your mind and you have completely neglected the development of your spirit. Paul puts it this way:

For if I pray in a tongue, my spirit prays, but my mind is unfruitful.

So what shall I do? I will pray with my spirit, but I will also pray with my understanding; I will sing with my spirit, but I will also sing with my understanding. (1 Cor. 14:14-15 NIV)

Paul is crystal clear in this passage. There is a kind of prayer that is not an intellectually driven activity. The mind is "unfruitful" meaning it is inactive. It is not productive. Instead, our spirits are active. How is the spirit active? It is active when we pray in tongues. Tongues are not, as some critics suggest, the practice of babbling and jumbling up words. That would actually be a mentally draining exercise. Tongues flow from our spirits. This does not mean our minds won't benefit. As we pray in the spirit, both our heart and our mind will come into alignment. Our heart will be filled with love, joy and peace (the fruit of the Spirit) and our minds will be focused on the truths of God. Speaking in tongues from our spirit will translate to prophesy in our understanding.

Some folks think the devil is just active out in the world where evil and ugly things happen. Yet the devil, or rather demons, actually operate closer to home than that. The enemy likes to set up camp in your mind and in your heart. He gains access through lies, and once he has access, he sets up strongholds. Many believers need deliverance because they have given over their mind and hearts to the enemy. Good theology and church involvement is no protection. Jesus was crucified by religious leaders who knew the scriptures, and who knew how to argue theologically, but their flesh-driven minds played right into the devil's hands. Satan used them to oppose the ministry of the Spirit through Jesus. The devil will always use fleshly religious people to attack the work of the Spirit. Paul says: "At that time the son born according to the flesh persecuted the son born by the power of the Spirit. It is the same now." (Gal. 4:29 NIV) It's always the same. Those driven by the flesh (self-sufficiency, legalism, human effort and achievement) will always oppose those led by the Spirit. To be led by the Spirit is the opposite of life in the flesh. Life in the Spirit begins by yielding to the Spirit. Life in the flesh is driven by our self-life. As Christians, our spirit has been renewed, but we need to bring every area of our life into alignment with our renewed spirit. Praying in tongues is praying in the spirit, and praying in the spirit leads us deeper into the things of the Spirit.

When I was preparing to write this book a well-meaning brother in the Lord told me that we don't need another book on tongues. He indicated that there was certainly no need for *me* to write a book on tongues (a humbling experience).

34

"Enough ink has been spilled." he said. That might be true. But I'm not looking for more ink to be spilled I'm looking for more fire to be stirred. It doesn't matter how much we think we *know* about the gifts. It doesn't matter how many books on the gifts that we have read. All that matters is this: are we burning with holy fire *now*? Are we stirring up the gift *now*? Are we using this gift of God to launch us into the heart of fellowship with the triune God *now*? Is the love of God soaring through our hearts because we are communing with God in our heavenly language *now*?

In seeking to understand how the devil attacks the gifts of the Holy Spirit, we can learn from the ministry of Edward Irving. Irving, a Church of Scotland minister in the 1800s, and a contemporary of Thomas Chalmers, that great figure of the Free Church of Scotland, was in many ways a pioneer of the recovery of Pentecost. Tragically, Irving was born in the wrong century. He was a generation too early. The Church of Scotland and indeed the wider churches were not yet ready for the ministry of the Holy Spirit. Irving was tried by the church courts and condemned for his ministry which taught about the baptism in the Holy Spirit and the gifts of tongues and prophecy.

I want to draw out a lesson from Irving's life. In his defence to the Presbytery, he warned them of the dangers of rejecting the baptism of the Holy Spirit, and the gifts of tongues and prophecy because it contradicted the church's traditions.

> Ah, if you will turn aside and say, There is nothing in the Church of Scotland for it; there is no authority for it, and we will not consider whether the thing is in Scripture or not – I tell you, you shall be withered as a church – I tell you the waters in your cisterns shall be dried up – I tell you, you shall have no pasture for your flocks – I tell you, your flocks shall pine away and die.[3]

This is a profound prophetic word. Almost two hundred years have passed since that prophecy was uttered. In many ways you could say that Irving's prophecy came to pass. The Church of Scotland has been dying a slow death for a very long time. The life is gone from parts of it. Many of the flock who once went to the church of Scotland have long since left and are finding pasture elsewhere. But that aside, the principle is beyond argument, if we reject the source of blessings, we will wither. Yet one of the main reasons that the church withers is because tradition is placed above scripture. In the next chapter we are going to take a journey through the Bible. Up until now I have mainly argued from experience. Let us now take a closer look at what the Bible

---

[3] *The Pentecostal Theology of Edward Irving*, Gordon Strachan, p163.

says about the work of the Spirit and speaking in tongues.

3 What does the Bible Say?

In this book I have been addressing believers who I presume have some understanding of what is meant by the phrase *speaking in tongues*. Whilst my primary aim is to encourage those who have received the gift but for whom it has perhaps become dormant, I also want to encourage others who perhaps reject or neglect the gifts to re-examine their position. At the same time there are limitations to every book. This book is not an in depth academic treatment of the subject of the baptism in the Spirit and speaking in tongues. If I were to attempt such a book, I wouldn't do it justice, and nor would this book achieve its purpose. This isn't a book for academics, this book is written with pastoral motivations and it is intended to have practical results – I hope non-tongue speaking readers will be stirred up to *receive* the gift of tongues, and I hope that tongue-speaking readers will *stir* up the gift they have already received.

The Book of Acts: A Pattern to Follow?

In order to gain an understanding of the baptism of the Holy Spirit we will look at the book of Acts and later the book of 1 Corinthians. However, before we do, let us deal with a common objection to this approach. Some critics of Pentecostal experience claim that the book of Acts cannot be considered normative, and is not intended for teaching. John MacArthur, for example, claims:

> Charismatics…craving the experiences described in Acts, have assembled a doctrinal system that views the extraordinary events of the early apostolic age as necessary hall marks of the Holy Spirit's working – tokens of spiritual power that are to be routinely expected by all Christians at a times.[4]

There is a degree of irony and inconstancy in MacArthur's argument here. As an evangelical and a Baptist, MacArthur himself is part of a movement that would not exist had the evangelical and Baptist forefathers not returned to the book of Acts. One of the greatest truths that led to the rediscovery of believer's baptism was the fact that nowhere in the book of Acts do we see infants being baptised. All who received water baptism were old enough to believe and repent.

---

[4] Charismatic Chaos, John MacArthur, p208.

Further, evangelical evangelism has also drawn its inspiration from the book of Acts. It was the book of Acts that led to the evangelical revivals that helped shift western Christians away from a Christendom mindset to a missional mindset. The evangelical brethren revivals and church planting movements drew their inspiration from Acts 2:42 (a description of the early church) and believed they were restoring the *biblical pattern*. Pentecostals have just continued that trajectory of restoration. They have realised that along with the recovery of doctrines like justification by faith, the priesthood of all believers, and believer's baptism, the church needed to recover the baptism and gifts of the Holy Spirit.

Further, Paul tells us that, "All scripture is God-breathed and is useful for teaching, rebuking, correcting and training in righteousness." (2 Timothy 3:16) In other words, we don't just learn from theological propositions like the ones that Paul expresses in many of his letters, we learn from the narrative texts of the Bible. This principle applies to the Gospels. In the Gospels we don't just learn from what Jesus taught, we learn from what Jesus did, and from what others did including the disciples and the Pharisees. The historical narrative helps us see how it was, and how it should be.

The real problem is not that Pentecostals draw from Acts

(Lukan texts), the real problem is that anti-charismatics like MacArthur filter everything through certain Pauline texts. A more biblical approach is to hold Paul, John, Luke and other New Testament writers in harmony. We shouldn't make the mistake of saying, "I follow Paul" whilst neglecting what Luke wrote. That is the kind of immaturity that Paul himself rebukes in his letters. Luke is an essential New Testament writer who helps us understand the work of the Spirit and the charismata and he does this both in his gospel, and in his sequel, the book of Acts.

Preliminary Issues surrounding Baptism in the Holy Spirit and Subsequence

One of the issues we will explore in the following passages is the issue of *subsequence*. In other words, the view that 'baptism in the Holy Spirit' is *distinct* from regeneration (new birth) and also (usually) takes place after a person is born again. This has always been a divisive topic within the church, and whilst I hold to the subsequence position, the aim of this book is not to persuade readers to accept that position. Neither is it the case that one must hold to the doctrine of subsequence in order to experience tongues or even an 'anointing' or 'empowering' of the Holy Spirit. There are many believers who do not hold to this interpretation of the Spirit's work in Acts, yet they have experienced both speaking in tongues and the Holy Spirit's power and presence. For a number of years, I was less persuaded by the argument of subsequence as put forward by a number of Pentecostal bible teachers, and it was not until I read 'Joy Unspeakable' by Martyn Lloyd Jones, that I was persuaded that not only was the doctrine of subsequence biblical, but it was also possible to hold the doctrine of subsequence alongside a reformed understanding of scripture and salvation. Who could accuse Martyn Lloyd Jones of heresy for his views on the Baptism of the Holy Spirit when he so clearly thundered the gospel of grace, in the power of the Holy Spirit?

With that being said, let us look at some key scriptures that are essential if we are to understand the work of the Holy Spirit and speaking in tongues.

The Baptism of the Spirit: A Promise of Jesus

Immediately following his resurrection from the dead, and prior to his ascension, Jesus exhorted his apostles and followers to wait until they received what God had promised before they launched out into mission.

I am going to send you what my Father has promised; but stay in the city until you have been clothed with power from on high." (Lk. 24:49 NIV)

It should be clear that the promise Jesus is referring to is the baptism of the Holy Spirit that had been prophesied by John the Baptist and many of the Old Testament prophets. To the water-drenched, repentant and spiritually hungry crowds, John said: "I have baptized you with water, but he will baptize you with the Holy Spirit." (Mark 1:8 ESV) The metaphors "clothed" and "baptise" are significant. Followers of Jesus were not to anticipate a few crumbs falling from heaven, they were to be immersed, covered, and engulfed in the Spirit's presence. Howard M. Ervin says: "The baptism in the Holy Spirit results in one being permeated by, and filled to overflowing with the presence and power of the Holy Spirit."[5] T.N. Turnbull describes Pentecost in this way: "Surging down with overwhelming might the Holy Spirit descended, and immersed and filled the disciples with mighty power, and great happenings took place as a result of that outpouring."[6] It should be clear to anyone that the baptism of the Holy Spirit is an all-consuming experience. This is what was promised.

Jesus again exhorts the apostles in a similar manner in Acts 1, the risen Christ says: "But you will receive power

---

[5] Howard M. Ervin, Spirit Baptism: A Biblical Investigation, p25.
[6] What God Hath Wrought, T.N. Turnbull, p154.

when the Holy Spirit has come upon you, and you will be my witnesses in Jerusalem and in all Judea and Samaria, and to the end of the earth." (Acts 1:8 ESV) Here Jesus makes it clear that the coming gift from the father is the Holy Spirit, and that his coming will empower them to testify of his death and resurrection.

The distinction between Regeneration and Spirit Baptism

Some believers confuse this experience of the Holy Spirit with conversion or salvation. Whilst the baptism in the Holy Spirit may take place at the same time as conversion, this is not always the case. It was certainly not the case for these followers of Jesus[7], and it was not the case for others whose experience is recorded in other places in the book of Acts. There is a difference between being born of the Holy Spirit and being baptised in the Holy Spirit. The first relates to regeneration (being born again) the second relates to empowerment for mission. The disciples were already born

---

[7] It is acknowledged that the first account of the Baptism of the Holy Spirit was unique in several ways. Pentecost was a transitionary event. In this way, Pentecost alone could not be considered normative for all believers post-Pentecost. Were it not for the fact that the Book of Acts records three other occasions where there was a delay between regeneration and Spirit Baptism, it would be difficult to argue the distinction. The facts are that there are other accounts where the baptism in the Spirit follows conversion. This is where the pattern emerges, and this is one of the key reasons why many interpreters of scripture (not just charismatics) have taught the doctrine of *subsequence*.

again. At what point? On this issue, I find Howard M. Ervin's position to be the most persuasive. Ervin, drawing on the work of Plummer, argues that the disciples were born again on resurrection day, when John's Gospel records what Ervin calls the "The Paschal Impartation of the Spirit." In John's gospel, Jesus met with the disciples on resurrection day: "And with that he breathed on them and said, "Receive the Holy Spirit." (Jn. 20:22 NIV) The *risen* Christ breathes on his disciples and tells them to receive the Holy Spirit. Salvation comes to us when we confess that Jesus is Lord and believe he has been raised from the dead (Romans 10). Here the disciples are transitioning from being Old Covenant followers of the Messiah, to becoming New Covenant believers. They see the risen Christ, they believe, they receive the Spirit. Jesus physically breathes upon them. Spirit means breath.

Just as God breathed into Adam in Eden but then died spiritually because of sin, Jesus is now reversing the curse. Jesus is bringing the disciples into the life of the New Covenant. This happens when we are born again. It happens when we believe on the risen Saviour. Ervin writes:

The resurrection day, therefore, marks the beginning of the new creation. As in the former creation, man received life by the breath of God, so at the beginning of the new creation His disciples received new, spiritual life – they were born again – by the breath of the risen Son of God that is not only the source, but also the pledge of that eternal life bestowed on all who subsequently "believe on the Son."[8]

Whilst scholars are divided, and always will be, over the exact moment the first disciples were born again, Ervin's argument is thoroughly grounded in a canonical view of the Bible. It takes seriously the historical accounts in John's Gospel, and helps us understand the significance of the Paschal receiving of the Holy Spirit. New Testament scholar A. Plummer makes the same case: "There was therefore a Paschal as distinct from a Pentecostal gift of the Holy Spirit, the one preparatory to the other." Understanding the significance of John's account, not only helps us understand when the disciples were 'born again', it also helps us understand why in Acts there is often a delay between people's conversion and their receiving the Spirit in the same manner the disciples in the Upper Room did. T.N. Turnbull explains the distinction between the two experiences, this way:

> This gift of the baptism of the Holy Spirit is quite distinct from the work done in our hearts at regeneration. At the New Birth the Holy Spirit quickens, and makes us alive spiritually, but the

---

[8] Howard M. Ervin, Spirit Baptism, p17.

New Testament never refers to this experience as the baptism of the Holy Spirit. On each of the occasions that the Holy Spirit was poured out in the Acts of the Apostles, it was on people who had already been regenerated.[9]

When Luke speaks of the promise of the Spirit, he is never describing the new birth, he is describing a further experience of the Spirit that will empower them for mission. It is a revelation of the crucified, buried and *risen* Christ that brings us into salvation and the new birth, it is a revelation of the *ascended* Christ, his outpoured Spirit and accompanying gifts that prepares us for mission.

So, the purpose of the Spirit's coming, from Luke's perspective, was not for regeneration, it was for empowerment. However, it is important that baptism in the Spirit is not reduced to the concept of receiving 'power to be a witness.' There is something deeper than power.

Martyn Lloyd Jones, along with many other Christians, shares this view that baptism in the Spirit, as defined by Luke, is a work of the Spirit that is *subsequent* to regeneration. It is a gift for believers.

What is the baptism of the Holy Spirit? Now there are some, as we have seen, who say that there is really no difficulty about this at all. They say it is simply a reference to regeneration and

---

[9] What God Hath Wrought, Turnbull, p155.

nothing else. It is what happens to people when they are regenerated and incorporated into Christ, as Paul teaches in 1 Corinthians 12:13: 'By one Spirit are we all baptized into one body' . . . Therefore, they say, this baptism of the Holy Spirit is simply regeneration.

But for myself, I simply cannot accept that explanation, and this is where we come directly to grips with the difficulty. I cannot accept that because if I were to believe that, I should have to believe that the disciples and the apostles were not regenerate until the Day of Pentecost — a supposition which seems to me to be quite untenable. In the same way, of course, you would have to say that not a single Old Testament saint had eternal life or was a child of God.[10]

If the baptism of the Holy Spirit is subsequent to regeneration, how then does a believer know he has received it? Lloyd Jones goes on to speak about the evidence of the baptism of the Spirit.

The mark, ultimately, and proof of whether we have received the Spirit or not is surely something that happens in the realm of our spiritual experience. You cannot read the New Testament accounts of the people to whom the Spirit came, these people upon whom He fell, or who received as the Galatian Christians and all these others had done, without realizing that the result was that their whole spirit was kindled.

---

[10] Martyn Lloyd Jones.

The Lord Jesus Christ became real to them in a way that He had never been before . . . the result was a great love for Christ shed abroad in their hearts by the Holy Spirit.[11]

The Baptism of the Spirit as a Divine Encounter

Pentecostal scholar, Simon Chan makes a similar argument to Lloyd Jones. Chan argues that Pentecostals have done a poor job of communicating the experience to the next generation. He notes that it has often been "narrowly defined as 'the enduement of power for life and service,' when in reality the baptism of the Spirit is "Nothing less than the 'revelation' of the triune God, a 'theophany' of the God of history and the eschaton." Apostolic pastor, and Pentecostal scholar, Jonathan Black makes a similar point, he says: "We must not lose sight of the fact that He is not only giving power, He is giving Himself."

In other words, at the heart of the baptism of the Spirit, there is a deep encounter with God. The baptism of the Spirit ought to be a deeply-life changing experience. Let's look at what happened to the disciples in the Upper Room.

Pentecost

The day of Pentecost is an important event, the promise of

---

[11] Lloyd Jones.

the Holy Spirit was for the waiting believers and through their witness it would be offered to all who would call on the name of the Lord. Acts 2 takes us to the point of climax. The disciples of Jesus, in obedience to his instructions, are *praying and waiting* for the promise of God in the Upper Room. In Acts 2 we read:

When the day of Pentecost came, they were all together in one place.

2 Suddenly a sound like the blowing of a violent wind came from heaven and filled the whole house where they were sitting.

3 They saw what seemed to be tongues of fire that separated and came to rest on each of them.

4 All of them were filled with the Holy Spirit and began to speak in other tongues as the Spirit enabled them. (Acts 2:1-4 NIV)

Notice that *all* of them were *filled* and *all of them* began to *speak in tongues*. T.N. Turnbull notes that:

So tremendous on the day of Pentecost was the impact of the Spirit of God upon the spirit of man that even his speech was changed. Men spoke as they never spoke before, for the simple reason that the Holy Spirit gave them utterance. Men found themselves with power to speak with other and unknown tongues. This is the scriptural pattern for believers receiving the baptism of the Holy Spirit for the whole church age.[12]

Turnbull makes two key points here. The first is that there is a pattern in Acts. In other words, whenever we see a group of people receive the baptism in the Spirit, the most consistent sign that follows is tongues. Before we look at Turnbull's reason for this, let us just take a moment to explore what is meant by speaking with tongues.

What is Speaking in Tongues?

What is speaking in tongues? The New Testament, on numerous occasions, refers to a phenomenon of people speaking in tongues. Speaking with tongues is *the Spirit-enabled ability to speak an unintelligible language*, sometimes referred to as a heavenly language, *but it can also refer to earthly foreign languages*, that have *not been taught or learned naturally*.[13] We first see this phenomenon here in Acts 2 when the Holy Spirit is initially poured out, but we will also see it on other occasions, in Acts, when people receive the Holy Spirit.

---

[12] What, Turnbull, p156.

[13] "The Greek word for 'tongue' is γλῶσσα, ης, ἡ and that is its literal definition. It means literally, the organ of speech." However, figuratively, it translates as "a religious technical term for glossolalia *tongues(-speaking)*, understood variously to be unintelligible ecstatic utterance (1C 14.2), heavenly language (1C 13.1), or foreign languages not learned through natural means by the speaker (AC 2.4)" *Friberg, Analytical Greek Lexicon*

The relationship between speaking tongues and Spirit Baptism

Jonathan Black observes that: "From the earliest days of the Pentecostal revivals, Pentecostals have seen a strong connection between the baptism in the Spirit and speaking other tongues."[14] This is not just because of what happened in Acts 2, (if that were the case why do we not expect the sound like a rushing wind and the tongues of fire too?) it is because of what happens in the other 'Pentecost' narratives within the book of Acts. Let's look at those narratives now.

The 'Samaritan Pentecost'

In Acts 8 we have a remarkable account of the what the church's evangelism and mission looked like.

> 5 Then Philip went down to the city of Samaria and preached Christ to them.
>
> 6 And the multitudes with one accord heeded the things spoken by Philip, hearing and seeing the miracles which he did.
>
> 7 For unclean spirits, crying with a loud voice, came out of many who were possessed; and many who were paralyzed

---

14 Black, Apostolic Theology, p461.

and lame were healed.

8 And there was great joy in that city.

9 But there was a certain man called Simon, who previously practiced sorcery in the city and astonished the people of Samaria, claiming that he was someone great,

10 to whom they all gave heed, from the least to the greatest, saying, "This man is the great power of God."

11 And they heeded him because he had astonished them with his sorceries for a long time.

12 But when they believed Philip as he preached the things concerning the kingdom of God and the name of Jesus Christ, both men and women were baptized.

13 Then Simon himself also believed; and when he was baptized he continued with Philip, and was amazed, seeing the miracles and signs which were done.

14 Now when the apostles who were at Jerusalem heard that Samaria had received the word of God, they sent Peter and John to them,

15 who, when they had come down, prayed for them that they might receive the Holy Spirit.

16 For as yet He had fallen upon none of them. They had only been baptized in the name of the Lord Jesus.

17 Then they laid hands on them, and they received the Holy Spirit. (Acts 8:5-17 NKJ)

There are so many points to draw out from this narrative. Firstly, we need to note that signs and wonders accompanied Philip's evangelistic ministry. Philip was not an apostle; he was an evangelist. We later read he had daughters who prophesied. From this we can clearly see that the supernatural gifts of the Spirit were not restricted to those who were 'apostles' and we also see that the gifts were manifest in the next generation.

Secondly, the account in Acts 8 demonstrates the doctrine of subsequence. In other words, baptism in the Holy Spirit did not occur when the people who heard Philip's preaching repented, believed and were baptised.

Some commentators argue that this was a special circumstance, and it was because the believers were Samaritans and there was a racial rift between Jews and Samaritans. However, the "special circumstance" argument begins to wear thin when it is applied to the believers on the Day of Pentecost, *and* the believers in Samaria, *and* later (as we shall soon see) the believers in Ephesus (Acts 19).

Thirdly, this scene in Acts 8 demonstrates that not only is the baptism in the Holy Spirit not identical to regeneration, but baptism in the Holy Spirit is recognised because of the signs that accompany it. If this were not the case, how would Philip and the apostles know that the believers in Samaria had not received the baptism of the Holy Spirit? If the baptism or filling with the Spirit is synonymous with conversion, why did they think that the Samaritans had not received the Spirit? Let's look at what happened after Philip preached. It says: "But when they believed Philip as he preached the things concerning the kingdom of God and the name of Jesus Christ, both men and women were baptized." (Acts 8:12 NKJ)

If we were to replace Philip with the average evangelical evangelist, that evangelist would have went home satisfied that his mission had been a success. The people had believed and were baptised. In reformed evangelicalism it's impossible to believe without the Holy Spirit. Faith is the evidence of regeneration. From an evangelical perspective, there is nothing in this situation to suggest that the Samaritans had not received the Holy Spirit. This proves a simple point: the early church did not see conversion as evidence of the baptism of the Spirit. A profession of faith and baptism was enough to identify a person as a believer, but it was not the evidence of the baptism of the Holy Spirit.

Acts 8 does not actually tell us specifically what the evidence that the Spirit had been received was. But it does suggest that it was something that could be observed. It was something that could be seen. Luke tells us, "Simon saw that through the laying on of the apostles' hands the Holy Spirit was given." (Acts 8:18 NKJ) What did Simon see? It must have been a supernatural sign because he wanted to buy it. The guy was obsessed with the supernatural, but for all the wrong reasons. This was a guy who had dabbled in occult power. He clearly saw a supernatural manifestation once the apostles laid hands on those who were wanting to receive the baptism in the Spirit. It is enough to conclude from this narrative that there can be a delay between regeneration and baptism in the Spirit, and that baptism in the Spirit is identified by something that can be seen. Some sort of supernatural physical evidence. To discover what that evidence is, we need to look at the other accounts of people being baptised by the Holy Spirit.

The 'Gentile Pentecost'

The next account of the baptism of the Holy Spirit we encounter is in Acts chapter 10. In this account God has been dealing with Peter's legalistic and nationalistic prejudice. He wants him to go and preach to Gentiles. As he is preaching to them, the Holy Spirit falls on them. What is significant is the experience is accompanied with signs.

44 While Peter was still speaking these words, the Holy Spirit fell upon all those who heard the word.

45 And those of the circumcision who believed were

astonished, as many as came with Peter, because the gift of the Holy Spirit had been poured out on the Gentiles also.

46 For they heard them speak with tongues and magnify God. Then Peter answered,

47 "Can anyone forbid water, that these should not be baptized who have received the Holy Spirit just as we have?"

48 And he commanded them to be baptized in the name of the Lord. Then they asked him to stay a few days. (Acts 10:44-48 NKJ)

This account in Acts 10 is significant for a few reasons. Although it does not show a delay between regeneration and Spirit baptism it shows us that the baptism in the Holy Spirit is recognised because of the sign that accompanies it. Notice how they recognise that the Spirit has been received:

The gift of the Holy Spirit had been poured out on the Gentiles also.

For they heard them speak with tongues and magnify God. Then Peter answered, "Can anyone forbid water, that these should not be baptized who have received the Holy Spirit just as we have?" (Acts 10:45-47 NKJ)

The reasoning is clear, the "those of the circumcision" recognise the Gentiles have received the Holy Spirit "FOR they heard them speak with tongues". Further they connect it to their own experience: "just as we have." This point is

57

reinforced because it is repeated later when Peter has to give an account to the Jewish believers in Acts 11.

> 15 "And as I began to speak, the Holy Spirit fell upon them, as upon us at the beginning.16 "Then I remembered the word of the Lord, how He said, 'John indeed baptized with water, but you shall be baptized with the Holy Spirit.'
>
> 17 "If therefore God gave them the same gift as *He gave* us when we believed on the Lord Jesus Christ, who was I that I could withstand God?" (Acts 11:15-17 NKJ)

So far we have seen three accounts where the Spirit has been received, in all three accounts the reception of the Spirit was recognised because of something that could be observed. On two of those occasions the sign that follows the baptism of the Holy Spirit is tongues. Let us now turn to the fourth account of Spirit baptism in the book of Acts.

The 'Ephesian Pentecost'

We now come to the ministry of the Apostle Paul. In Acts 19 he comes across a group of disciples of John the Baptist.

> And it happened, while Apollos was at Corinth, that Paul, having passed through the upper regions, came to Ephesus. And finding some disciples
>
> 2 he said to them, "Did you receive the Holy Spirit when you believed?" So they said to him, "We have not so much as heard whether there is a Holy Spirit."

³ And he said to them, "Into what then were you baptized?" So they said, "Into John's baptism."

⁴ Then Paul said, "John indeed baptized with a baptism of repentance, saying to the people that they should believe on Him who would come after him, that is, on Christ Jesus."

⁵ When they heard *this*, they were baptized in the name of the Lord Jesus.

⁶ And when Paul had laid hands on them, the Holy Spirit came upon them, and they spoke with tongues and prophesied.

⁷ Now the men were about twelve in all. (Acts 19:1-7 NKJ)

In attempting to discern their current spiritual condition, Paul asks them: "Did you receive the Holy Spirit when you believed?" Jonathan Black makes the point, "The very fact that Paul could ask such a question shows that he considered the baptism in the Holy Spirit something distinct from conversion, for if all Christians were automatically baptised in the Holy Spirit at the moment of conversion, this question wouldn't make any sense."[15] There has been disagreement amongst scholars as to whether or not these believers are in fact Christians. I personally don't think they were. They were disciples of John who were yet to fully understand who Jesus was. This is why Paul then explains to them John's message about Jesus. Once they accept this, they are baptised into the name of Jesus. In other words, they

---

[15] Apostolic, Black, p459.

received the baptism in water that all disciples of Christ are to receive. Again, all evangelical evangelists would stop at this point, but not Paul. Paul then lays his hands upon them, and as he does the Spirit falls upon them and they speak in tongues, all 12 of them.

Acts 19 shows us a few things, firstly, in Paul's mind, believing in Jesus was not synonymous with the baptism of the Holy Spirit, secondly, even when Paul leads them to Christ and baptises them in water they are still not yet baptised in the Holy Spirit, thirdly, the baptism in the Holy Spirit happens when Paul lays his hands on them (just like what happened to the Samaritans), and fourthly, the sign of the Spirit's presence is that they speak in tongues and prophesy.

Evaluating the Evidence

Having looked at the main accounts of the baptism with the Holy Spirit in the book of Acts we have seen the following pattern: in three out of four occasions there is a delay between conversion and the baptism of the Holy Spirit, on all four occasions there is some sort of sign that can be observed to confirm that the Spirit has been received, in three out of four of these occasions the sign is tongues (and on one occasion prophesying is also mentioned), on two occasions the baptism of the Holy Spirit is received when hands are laid on the recipients and on two occasions God sovereignly pours out his Spirit.

Overall, we should understand that there is a degree of both unity and diversity in the way the Spirit works. In terms of 'signs' that accompany the baptism in the Holy Spirit, tongues are the sign that is mentioned most consistently. All who were filled with the Holy Spirit on the day of Pentecost received tongues, as did the Gentiles who Peter preached to and as did the disciples at Ephesus. Whilst the Samaritan example did not cite tongues specifically, it is not unreasonable to infer, from the other accounts, that what Simon 'saw' was tongues and possibly the gift of prophecy.

The important thing to take away from this is to understand that there is more to the Christian walk than our initial profession of faith in Jesus. To reduce Christianity to "accepting Jesus" and being "assured of heaven" is one of the great errors of evangelicalism. Too many believers are stuck in a rut. They see their profession of faith as a ticket to heaven, and they think their profession of faith is the finish line when in fact it is only the starting line. The Christian faith is a journey. Initiation to the Christian faith is a process, and that process involves repentance, faith, water baptism and the filling/receiving/baptism of the Holy Spirit.

One of the reasons why the modern church lacks the power and vibrancy of the early church is because we have neglected the foundations of the faith. Likewise, our Christian life will not be as fruitful as it should be if our foundations are not right. This book is primarily about speaking in tongues, but there is no point in seeking tongues if your Christian faith is insecure because your foundations are not right. Blessing comes from obeying the revelation of God that's in his word.

Before seeking tongues, we need to first make sure we are born again and filled with the Holy Spirit. Your first need may not be tongues at all. Your first need might be salvation. It may be that you need to obey the command to be baptised in water as a believer. Likewise, it may be that you need to be filled with the Holy Spirit. Once you are filled with the Spirit you may find that tongues comes with the package.

In the following chapter, we are going to look more closely at the relationship between tongues and the baptism of the Holy Spirit. Having looked at the biblical accounts, we will look at historical accounts, and then seek to understand how we should understand the subject today. Likewise, we will seek to understand the relationship between tongues and the baptism of the Holy Spirit and what that should mean for us today.

4 Tongues and Baptism in the Spirit Today?

In chapter three we surveyed some of the key Spirit baptisms in Acts and argued that regeneration and conversion are not synonymous with the baptism in the Holy Spirit (the doctrine of subsequence). We also noted that the baptism in the Holy Spirit in every account was connected with some sort of sign, normally tongues but sometimes prophecy (the doctrine of "initial evidence" or "signs following". In this chapter we will explore both of these views in light of church history, and contemporary experience. The main purpose of this chapter is to explore whether the church has considered it normative to believe in a subsequent experience of the Holy Spirit and to understand how Pentecostals understand tongues in relation to the doctrine of subsequence.

Subsequence in Church History

Many evangelical critics of the teaching on the baptism of the Holy Spirit oppose the doctrine of subsequence with a fierce hostility. Claims of "heresy" and "falsehood" abound. It is feared that such a teaching is a modern innovation that has no grounding in scripture or church history. However, the fact is that it is *the evangelical position* that is novel. It is the evangelical position that is divorced from church history. The distinction between Spirit baptism and conversion is a view that has been taught by the church fathers, Roman Catholics, Anglicans, Greek Orthodox, a number of the Puritans, Methodists, Holiness Churches, Pentecostals, and giants of church history such as John Wesley, (Anglican), Charles Finney (Presbyterian), Edward Irving (Presbyterian), R.A. Torrey (Evangelical) and Martyn Lloyd Jones (Calvinistic Methodist). Now, I'm not claiming that these all held identical views, they didn't. However, their testimony is that there is a further work of the Spirit that is subsequent to conversion.

The church father Tertullian, in his teaching baptism, before he became a Montanist, wrote the following:

Therefore, you blessed ones, for whom the grace of God is waiting, when you come up from the most sacred bath of the new birth, when you spread out your hands for the first time in your mother's house with your brethren, ask your father, ask your Lord, for the special gift of his inheritance, the distributed charisms, which form an additional, underlying feature [of baptism]. Ask, he says, and you shall receive. In fact, you have sought, and you have found: you have knocked, and it has been opened to you.[16]

The great Puritan, Richard Sibbes taught that the sealing of the Spirit, mentioned by Paul in his letter to the Ephesians, was: a *"superadded work"* and *"superadded confirmation"*.

Thomas Goodwin, also argued that the "sealing of the Spirit" was separate from the new birth:

Light beyond the light of ordinary faith....The sealing of the Holy Spirit is an immediate assurance by a heavenly and divine light of a divine authority, which the Holy Ghost sheddeth in a man's heart, (not having relation to grace wrought or anything in a man's self,) whereby he sealeth him up to the day of redemption. ... It is the next thing to heaven. ... You can have no more until you come thither.

Martyn Lloyd Jones, in his book 'Joy Unspeakable' states:

You cannot be a Christian without having the Holy Spirit in you. But – and here is the point – I am asserting at the same time that you can be a believer, that you can have the Holy Spirit dwelling in you, and still not be baptised with the Holy

---

[16] McDonnell and Montague, *Christian Initiation,* p98.

Spirit.[17]

Contemporary Roman Catholic, William J. O'Shea emphasises the further work of the Spirit which is expected to be realised in the sacrament of confirmation:

> It was his own Spirit that Jesus poured forth abundantly on Pentecost, with the mission of continuing among men on the mystery of the incarnation. This the Spirit poured out on us in confirmation. Its mission in us is the same: to bring us to the full measure of the age of Christ.
>
> Just as Jesus needed the presence and action of the Spirit to realise to the full God the Father's design in him, we need the same Spirit to realise the divine plan is that we should be conformed to Christ, be made in his likeness. ... The difference between baptism and confirmation is the difference between giving life and enabling that life to reveal its full potential. Confirmation gives us the power to be what we already are in baptism.[18]

Heidi Baker, in her PhD thesis which explores the history of glossolalia and Spirit baptism concludes the following:

> We may argue that many traditions in church history have spoken of an experience of Spirit baptism, and therefore Pentecostalism need not be considered unorthodox in its belief in Spirit baptism as subsequent to conversion initiation. Virtually all Christian denominations have asserted that there

---

[17] 'Joy Unspeakable', Martyn Lloyd Jones, p23.
[18] Heidi Baker, PHD Thesis.

some difference between the Holy Spirit's work of regeneration and the Holy Spirit's work of baptism.[19]

Signs of Spirit Baptism

The unique difference between the Pentecostal emphasis on subsequence and the various doctrines of subsequence within other branches of the church is that Pentecostals have connected the subsequent receiving of the baptism of the Holy Spirit with the gifts of the Holy Spirit, and tongues in particular. However, even within Pentecostalism there is a diversity of views on the relationship between tongues and Spirit baptism. In particular, it is important to understand the difference between North American Pentecostalism and European Pentecostalism. Keith Warrington notes:

> Many Pentecostals associate the gift of speaking in tongues with the baptism of the Spirit, viewing it as the initial evidence, particularly among Pentecostals in the USA. ... However, other Pentecostals do not view tongues as the initial evidence of the baptism in the Spirit.[20]

Jonathan Black echoes this fact from a UK Pentecostal perspective:

> Some Pentecostal denominations hold strongly to a doctrine of tongues as the initial evidence of the baptism in the Spirit (e.g.

---

[19] Heidi Baker, PHD.
[20] Warrington, Pentecostal Theology, p120-121.

the Assemblies of God), while others, in their confessions of faith, speak somewhat less dogmatically of 'signs following' the baptism in the Holy Spirit (e.g. the Apostolic Church and the Elim Pentecostal Church).[21]

The distinction that Black mentions can be seen clearly in each UK Pentecostal denomination's statement of Faith. The UK AoG's position states:

> We believe in the baptism in the Holy Spirit as an enduement of the believer with power for service, the essential, biblical evidence of which is the speaking with other tongues as the Spirit gives utterance.

Notice that speaking in tongues is regarded as being "essential" and the "bible evidence" of having received the baptism of the Holy Spirit. On the other hand, the Apostolic Church expresses their understanding of the baptism of the Holy Spirit this way, they state that they believe in:

> The baptism of the Holy Spirit for believers with supernatural signs, empowering the church for its mission in the world.

The scriptural evidence that both denominations appeal to is the exact same, it is the four narratives in Acts that we looked at in chapter three. The distinction between the two positions is important though. But what does the difference of the Apostolic Church position mean in practice? Jonathan Black, again, is helpful here.

---

[21] Black, Apostolic.

'Signs following' still sees a very close connection between speaking in tongues and the baptism of the Holy Spirit. Speaking in tongues is still held to be the scriptural evidence of the baptism, or the God witness of the Baptism of the Spirit, and so the 'signs following' are expected to include speaking in tongues.[22]

Black unpacks further the key distinction between the two positions:

The difference between 'signs following' and 'initial physical evidence' is not the connection between the baptism in the Holy Spirit and speaking in tongues, but rather a rejection of the American 'initial physical evidence' position that 'if there is no manifestation of tongues, then there is no Spirit baptism.' Instead, the Apostolic position is that speaking tongues is considered to be 'the overflowing sign' of the baptism in the Holy Spirit. We are not just to assume that we have received in faith without any tangible experience. The experiential nature of the baptism means that there will be signs following.[23]

Jonathan Black argues further:

Thus, the difference between the 'initial physical evidence' position and the 'signs following' position, is in the necessary timing of speaking in tongues. Those who advocate 'signs following' say that tongues is the normal overflowing sign of the Spirit's fullness, but this might not be at exactly at the same

---

[22] Black, Apostolic, p464.
[23] Black, Apostolic, p464.

time, and the tongues may follow later. This position avoids the danger of confusing the baptism of the Spirit with nothing other than the ability to speak in tongues.[24]

Apostolic Church UK and Tongues as a Sign

Whilst the Apostolic Church's understanding still sees a connection with tongues and the baptism of the Holy Spirit, and still considers tongues to be normative, it does not go so far as to say that *if there is no tongues, the person has not been baptised in the Holy Spirit.* Extracts from early Apostolic Church leaders confirm this. W.A.C. Rowe says:

> We do not assert that a person may not receive the baptism of the Holy Spirit without the initial sign of speaking with other tongues... we realise that there are other signs of the Spirit filled life, such as say, the fruit of the Spirit may be termed signs or indications of the Spirit's abiding within."[25]

Likewise, an Apostolic International Council Meeting in 1932 records:

> Undoubtedly it is true that there is a possibility for you to have real fullness of the Holy Ghost, and that fullness not rightly directed to the utterance of tongues ... it has not come out in tongues, but the fullness has come in ... Our teaching is that they should expect speaking in tongues, but the Holy

---

[24] Black Apostolic.
[25] William A.C. Rowe, One Lord, One Faith, p135.

Ghost may work in another way.[26]

In my understanding, this approach is a sensible, and biblical way to bridge the tensions between seeing the biblical 'signs following' that accompany the baptism in the Holy Spirit, whilst recognising, in experience, there is a diversity in the Spirit's working. This approach acknowledges the predominant place that speaking in tongues holds in the Acts Spirit baptism narratives, whilst recognising that the Spirit's presence can be identified in other ways. It is not going so far as some expressions of the charismatic movement have gone and made speaking in tongues *optional* or *of minimal importance*, but equally it attempts to avoid pastoral insensitivity to people who may not have experienced tongues, but whose lives have clear marks of the Spirit's grace and power at work.

Further, the position held by Black, the Apostolic Church, and Elim is closer to the understanding of Spirit baptism and tongues that marked the early days of the charismatic movement. At the start of the charismatic movement the experience and explanation of Spirit baptism was almost indistinguishable from the earlier Pentecostal experience and explanation. Dennis J. Bennett, the spearhead of the charismatic renewal, when he was being prayed for to

---

[26] Black, Apostolic, p464-465.

receive the baptism of the Holy Spirit said: "Remember, I want this nearness of God you have, that's all; I'm not interested in speaking with tongues!" Those praying for Dennis replied: "All we can tell you is that it came with the package!" And come with the package it did. In fact, Bennett's account of the renewal very much revolves around people discussing and receiving tongues and the baptism in the Holy Spirit. Likewise, one of the most famous accounts of the charismatic renewal demonstrates the central place that tongues held in the movement in the title of the book: 'They Speak with Other Tongues' by John L. Sherrill.

The Evolution of Pentecostalism

Whilst the Charismatic and Pentecostal movements have continued to grow since the early days of Pentecostalism at the turn of the 20th century, and the height of the charismatic renewal in 60s and 70s, the reality is the landscape has changed as have theological understandings.

I think this has happened for several reasons. Firstly, 'The Third Wave' gave rise to a new form of charismatic evangelicalism. John Wimber, and Peter Wagner were very much at the heart of this movement. Unlike the Pentecostalism and Charismatic and Pentecostal movements, the Third Wave attempted to reconcile classical evangelical theology with the gifts and power of the Holy Spirit. Folks in the Third Wave tend to hold to the evangelical view that baptism in the Holy Spirit occurs at conversion, but there can be multiple anointings or empowering encounters that a Christian can receive and with these encounters the Holy Spirit releases spiritual gifts.

With the passing of time, and the dying out of the more traditional expressions of evangelicalism and Pentecostalism, the Third Wave approach has gained popularity. In many ways, there is a lot that's attractive in the Third Wave approach: it diminishes dogmatic doctrinal divisions, it actively attempts to unite evangelicals and charismatics by promoting the 'radical middle', and it attempts to remove labels and allow for diversity of experience.

The second factor that has arisen in recent years is the emergence of a more robust Pentecostal, Charismatic, and Third Wave Theology. Pentecostalism was largely a grass roots movement amongst primarily uneducated preachers. This is not to diminish their spirituality, it's just a fact. Pentecostals lived their theology; they were not academic theologians. At that time most of the theological institutions were steeped in Higher Criticism and most seminaries were producing liberal preachers. For this reason, Pentecostals were suspicious of an academic approach to theology. However, in recent years Pentecostal theology, and seminaries are experiencing explosive growth. Consequently, a number of leading Pentecostal theologians no longer hold to the doctrines of subsequence, or tongues as initial evidence, or many of the early Pentecostal doctrines (Gordon Fee being one of the most influential). As a result of both the evolving diversity of Pentecostalism and Pentecostal theology, there is now a plethora of deeply developed academic interpretations of Pentecostalism. Consequently, with more and more Pentecostal pastors being educated in seminaries, less Pentecostal pastors are now holding to the early Pentecostal doctrines of Spirit baptism.

The outcome of the emergence of the Third Wave, the rise of Pentecostal theologies, and the prevailing culture of relativism in society, has, I think, created a degree of theological relativism within the Pentecostal and Charismatic movements. In contrast to the early Pentecostal Pioneers who spoke with simplicity, conviction and power, we now have complexity, apathy, and a lack of power.

However, we also need to remember that the early Pentecostals did not shake the world upside down because they downplayed doctrine and focused on a vague experience of the Holy Spirit. The early Pentecostals were sold out on a very small number of foundational truths. They believed in sin, final judgement, the atonement of Christ, salvation by grace, the need for holiness, and a baptism of power for the purpose of seeing the lost saved from hell before Jesus returns. In simpler terms, they held to a four-square gospel: Jesus was the saviour, the healer, the baptiser in the Holy Spirit and the soon coming King. The point is this, the early Pentecostals simply believed the Bible and preached what they saw. They expected to receive all that God had promised. The result was they were shaken by the power of God, and they in turn shook the world.

Pentecostalism was an *Ad Fontes* movement: back to the sources. Just like the early disciples in the book of Acts. The Holy Spirit took hold of a prayerful, surrendered and faith-full group of believers. They were baptised in fire, and they set the world ablaze.

No one wants to split hairs over doctrine, no one wants to emphasise dogmatic doctrinal divisions, we all want to build bridges across the theological barriers, however, I can't help but think that there is a clear correlation between the shift away from foundational truths and the overall decline of Pentecostal experience within the Pentecostal and Charismatic movements. Warrington writes:

There has been a decrease in the numbers of Pentecostals who claim to have experienced the baptism in the Spirit, especially in the West, and this is coupled by concerns that the experience is only encouraged to a limited extent by Pentecostal leaders. … although the number of converts has increased in AoG churches in the USA, the numbers of those who experienced the baptism of the Holy Spirit have plateaued for the 25 years; currently for every five converts, there is one Spirit baptism. The danger facing contemporary Pentecostalism is that the experience of the Spirit as encountered by those in the early church is largely irrelevant to many Pentecostals, compounded by the fact that the experiences of the early Pentecostals generations have also largely been forgotten. Few people are modelling the dynamic transformation following the baptism in the Spirit; for too many, the models died decades ago.[27]

Apostolic Networks

Whilst Warrington identifies a decrease of Pentecostal and Charismatic activity, which he connects with an absence of a dynamic Spirit-empowered leadership that was once characteristic of the Pentecostal movements, it is important to note whilst this may be reflective of the historic Pentecostal denominations, it is not always the case elsewhere. Pentecostal scholar, William K. Kay has carried

---

[27] Warrington, Pentecostal, p124.

out extensive research of what has been identified as the emerging Apostolic Networks. These networks emerged out of the restorationist movement (the stream of the Charismatic movement that broke away from the mainstream church in order to better facilitate the renewal.)

Kay's study demonstrates two things, firstly, it highlights a number of contemporary leaders (or apostolic figures) who have emerged as a result of a transforming experience with the Holy Spirit and his gifts. Kay surveys the apostolic ministries of key figures such as: Bryn Jones who pioneered Covenant Ministries International; Terry Virgo and New Frontiers; Barney Coombs and Salt and Light; Tony Morton and CNET; Gerald Coates and Pioneer, Andrew Owen and Destiny Churches and many more. All of these figures were impacted by the baptism of the Holy Spirit and all of them have been instrumental in establishing an apostolic network.

Secondly, it demonstrates that whilst the doctrine of the baptism of the Holy Spirit and speaking in tongues is in decline in the older Pentecostal denominations, this is not necessarily true for the newer Apostolic Networks.

In terms of baptism in the Holy Spirit within the Apostolic Networks, Kay records that "95.8% say, 'I believe there is a distinct Christian experience that might be called, "the baptism in the Spirit" and 87% believe that the 'baptism in the Holy Spirit' is evidenced by 'signs following'."" Kay further notes that "the vast majority (94%) of these leaders believe that speaking in tongues is a form of private prayer and nearly 98% believe that speaking in tongues is an edifying experience."[28]

The Cycle of Renewal and Decay

I think what we see here is that the Lord is always in the business of renewing his church. Alongside the institutional church, throughout church history, there have always been renewal movements. When the western church became embroiled with the state, it set in motion a long chain of events that would take the church far away from its original purpose. Eventually the church drifted so far away that God raised up reformers like Martin Luther. Yet even the reformation needed to be reformed. Even the reformation became institutional. So, in every generation God has been restoring truth that has been lost, and re-igniting truth that has gone stale.

The reformation restored the doctrine of justification by faith, and the primary place of the scriptures, the Anabaptists and Baptists restored believer's baptism, the Holiness people restored sanctification, and the Pentecostals

---

[28] William, K. Kay,, Apostolic Networks, p320-321.

restored Spirit baptism, speaking in tongues, and the ministry of apostles and prophets. But even Pentecostalism has struggled with what Max Webber calls, "the routinization of charisma". In other words, Pentecostalism, having been a powerful movement in the past has not avoided the process of shifting from movement to museum.

Consequently, God breathed fresh life again to his church in the Charismatic renewal, and in the Third Wave, and also in the Apostolic Networks. Whilst each of these movements has looked slightly different and whilst each have slightly different theological understandings, all have striking similarities: they all place an emphasis on the baptism, or empowering of the Holy Spirit with 'signs following'. Further, tongues, however they are understood in relation to the baptism, are always considered to be an important factor in the devotional life and strengthening of believers.

Now that we have come full circle to tongues, we will now turn to the New Testament to look at the Apostle Paul and his teaching on the baptism in the Holy Spirit and speaking in tongues.

5 Was Paul Charismatic?

The Apostle Paul is the favoured New Testament writer among reformed and evangelical churches. This is not surprising as it was Paul's letter to the Romans which brought the young Roman Catholic priest, Martin Luther, to an understanding of justification by faith. Consequently, much of Paul's writing has been interpreted through this reformation lens of justification by faith. In more recent years, a deeper appreciation for Paul's experience and theology of the Spirit has emerged to the forefront. Gordon Fee's classic work, *God's Empowering Presence*: *The Holy Spirit in the Letter of Paul* is a case in point. In his introduction Fee argues that he was burdened to write the book because Paul's emphasis on the Spirit has largely been neglected.

The crucial role of the Holy Spirit in Paul's life and thought – as the dynamic, experiential reality, of the Christian life – is often either overlooked, or given mere lip service. ... I am equally convinced that the Spirit in Paul's experience and theology was always thought of in terms of the personal presence of God. The Spirit is God's way of being present, powerfully present, in our lives and communities as we await the consummation of the Kingdom of God. ... Paul also understood the Spirit in terms of God's empowering presence: whatever else, for Paul, the Spirit was an experienced reality.[29]

Various Biblical Terms for Spirit Baptism

The book of Acts uses a number of phrases to describe the experience that we have identified as the baptism in the Holy Spirit. The Epistles on the other hand, explain, in detail, what the book of Acts describes. In Acts we see people being converted; in the Epistles we learn what it means to be converted. In Acts we see people receiving the Holy Spirit and tongues, in the Epistles we discover what that means. Before we look at Paul's teaching in the Epistles, it's important to note the fluidity of language that Luke has already used to describe the experience of the Holy Spirit. Some of these descriptions are:

- 'Baptised with the Holy Spirit' (Acts 1:5)

---

[29] Gordon Fee, *God's Empowering Presence*, xxi.

- 'The promise of the Father' (Acts 1:4)
- The Holy Spirit 'coming upon' believers (Acts 1:8)
- 'The Holy Spirit fell upon' Acts (10:44)
- 'Filled with the Holy Spirit' (Acts 2:4)
- 'Received the Holy Spirit' (Acts 10:47)

Did Paul Understand Spirit Baptism as Regeneration?

With that said, let us now look at Paul's teaching on the baptism of Holy Spirit. One of the primary verses, is 1 Cor. 12:13. This is a key verse because it is the only place where Paul uses the phrase *'baptised* in one Spirit' Paul writes: For in one Spirit we were all baptized into one body-- Jews or Greeks, slaves or free-- and all were made to drink of one Spirit. (1 Cor. 12:13 ESV)

The primary point that Paul is dealing with in this verse is the unity of the body of Christ. Whilst there are different members, who make up different nationalities, or social backgrounds, there is one Holy Spirit into whom they have been baptised, and there is one church into which they have been incorporated – the body of Christ. Paul was correcting division in the local church, and in this verse he is exploring the relationship between the Holy Spirit and the union between the believers and the church which is Christ's body. Later, Paul will build on this concept and explain the relationship between the Holy Spirit, the gifts of the Holy Spirit and the church.

It's also important to understand the structure of this verse. This is an example of Hebrew parallelism, where two sentences are set in parallel in order to convey key truths. The Psalms are full of this kind of parallelism. The phrases that run parallel are:

For in one Spirit we were all baptized into one body
and all were made to drink of one Spirit.

Scholars have debated what kind of parallelism is being used. Some think it is *synonymous parallelism* (the two statements express the exact same truth) others think it is *synthetic parallelism* (they express a similar truth, but the second statement reveals a further truth). I tend to be of the view that it is synthetic parallelism. This is also the view that the reformers took. Those who hold to this view have not always agreed on what two distinct truths are being expressed. The reformers, building on the interpretations of many Catholic writers thought that the first statement was a reference to regeneration by water baptism, and the second statement was a reference to the Lord's Supper – the thought being there is a connection between drinking from the communion cup, and drinking from the Spirit.

The main issue surrounding this verse is that a number of

evangelicals associate Paul's use of the phrase 'baptised into one body' with regeneration. Consequently, if regeneration is really baptism in the Holy Spirit, then there is no need for believers to seek a subsequent baptism in the Holy Spirit. Consequently, evangelicals who understand initial saving faith (regeneration) and Spirit-baptism to be synonymous, and Roman Catholics who view water baptism and regeneration as synonymous, both use this verse to argue against the idea that baptism in the Holy Spirit is distinct and subsequent to regeneration.

Does Paul's use of the phrase that all believers are "baptised" in "one Spirit" into the "one body" serve the death knell for any claims that the baptism of the Holy Spirit does not take place at conversion? Lloyd Jones doesn't think so.

You cannot be a Christian without being regenerate. You cannot be a Christian without being a member of the body of Christ. Every Christian is baptised into the body of Christ, the apostle tells us in verse 13: 'By one Spirit we are all baptised into one body, whether we be Jews or Gentiles, whether we be bond or free; and have been made to drink into one Spirit. The Spirit is in every Christian. 'If any man have not the Spirit of Christ, he is none of his.'

That is what this statement is saying. But it has no reference whatsoever to the doctrine of the baptism with the Spirit or the blessing which comes to those who have been baptised with the Spirit. So this verse, which some people seem to think is crucial, not only does not contradict what we have been saying, but tends to prove it, and that to the very hilt, because we have seen so clearly and in so many different places that there are people described in Acts who have believed and have been baptised but still the apostles had to lay their hands upon them before they received the gift of the Holy Spirit.[30]

Lloyd Jones' understanding of the distinction between Luke's and Paul's use of the term is shared by a number of scholars and pastors. John Piper, a reformed Baptist pastor, also shares this view:

It's important that we clarify the meaning of biblical terms like "baptism in (or with) the Holy Spirit" because it is a biblical term. It's part of Christian experience.

What I'm going to suggest is that the way Paul uses the phrase in 1 Corinthians 12:13 and the way Luke uses the phrase (or Jesus reported by Luke) in Acts 1:5 are not the same. That's my basic premise, which would avoid a lot of confusion if people bought this. So you can check it out for yourself.

This means that when we ask, "What does the phrase 'baptism in (or baptism with) the Holy Spirit' mean?" we have to ask, "Are you talking about Paul's use or Luke's use as he quotes Jesus?" They're not contradictory. I'm not arguing that

---

[30] Jones, *Joy*, p335.

there's any conflict. I'm saying they use the same words in different ways. They use the same phrase in different ways.[31]

Leaving aside the technical details in 1 Cor 12:13, it's also important to note the experiential language in both phrases in this verse. 'Baptised' has the sense of being immersed and 'drink' carries the sense of refreshment. Both phrases are experiential. Regarding the experiential emphasis in Paul, Fee writes:

Paul makes a clear connection between the Spirit and the experience of power. ... The Spirit was not only *experienced* in conversion, but was experienced in a *dynamic*, undoubtedly visible way. This is precisely why Paul appeals to the Spirit, the lavish experience of the Spirit, to make his points in both Gal 3: 2-4 and 1 Cor 12:13. ... Paul does not see life in the Spirit as the result of a single experience of the Spirit at conversion. The Spirit is the key to all of Christian life, and frequently Paul implies there are further, ongoing appropriations of the Spirit's empowering. For Paul life in the Spirit begins at conversion; at the same time that experience is both dynamic and renewable.[32]

Jonathan Black writes: The baptism of the Holy Spirit is not an invisible experience. Unlike justification, which we

---

[31] https://www.desiringgod.org/interviews/what-is-the-baptism-of-the-holy-spirit
[32] Fee, God's *Empowering*, p864.

cannot see, the baptism of the Spirit is experiential in nature.[33]

However we interpret the two phrases in 1 Cor. 12:13, it is clear that Paul associates the receiving of the Holy Spirit with an experience. Further it is incredibly unlikely that Paul is arguing against the doctrine of subsequence because Paul's own filling/baptism with the Holy Spirit occurred three days after his conversion on the Damascus Road. Having encountered the ascended Christ on the road to Damascus, Paul was converted to Christ and his life was set on a new trajectory. Whilst remaining blind for three days, the Lord calls a disciple named Ananias to minister to Paul.

> And Ananias went his way and entered the house; and laying his hands on him he said, "Brother Saul, the Lord Jesus, who appeared to you on the road as you came, has sent me that you may receive your sight and be filled with the Holy Spirit." (Acts 9:17 NKJ)

It's clear from Paul's own experience, and his ministry to the disciples in Ephesus that Paul did not see the filling or baptism with the Holy Spirit as synonymous with conversion. He prayed for the Ephesian disciples to receive the Holy Spirit through the laying of hands after their profession of faith and baptism in water. Likewise, he

---

[33] Black, Apostolic, p460.

himself was not filled with the Holy Spirit until three days after his conversion, and this baptism with the Holy Spirit came as a result of hands being laid on him, just like the Samaritans and just like the Ephesians.

What about 'signs following' and tongues in relation to Paul's baptism with the Holy Spirit? Again, whilst Luke does not state that tongues, or other signs, manifested immediately when Paul was filled with the Holy Spirit, we know that they did. Luke records: "Now God worked unusual miracles by the hands of Paul, (Acts 19:11 NKJ) and Paul himself writes to the Corinthian church: "I thank God that I speak in tongues more than all of you." (1 Cor. 14:18 ESV) In regards, to the relationship between 1 Cor 12:13 and Paul's own experience of the Holy Spirit, Ervin writes:

> In the light of his own experience of conversion and Spirit-filling, what did Paul mean in 1 Cor 12:13? The answer is obvious. One needs but to recall that Paul was converted on the Damascus road in his encounter with the risen Christ...and three days later he was filled with/baptised in the Holy Spirit when Ananias laid his hands upon him in the name of Jesus. It is apparent then, that the Spirit's activity in conversion was not terminal in Paul's experience. His personal Pentecost followed his conversion by three days.[34]

---

[34] *Ervin, Spirit Baptism*, p37.

Galatians and the Spirit and miracles

Paul's letter to the Galatians is a letter that is saturated in references to the Holy Spirit. In the letter, Paul is seeking to bring correction to a wayward church which is drifting from its sure footing in the gospel of grace and is coming under the spell of legalists who demand that the gentiles should be circumcised to show that they truly belong to God. Paul's argument is clear, the Holy Spirit, not circumcision, is the sign that people belong to the covenant people of God. Further, the Spirit is received by faith, not by keeping the law. Paul appeals to their present experience to assure them they have God's favour because of their faith, they don't need to be circumcised.

Yet in this midst of his correction, Paul makes a striking point, he points to their *present experience* as *evidence of the Spirit's* work in their midst. Paul asks them: "Therefore He who supplies the Spirit to you and works miracles among you, *does He do it* by the works of the law, or by the hearing of faith?" (Gal. 3:5 NKJ) It's a rhetorical question. The answer Paul expects them to understand is that the Spirit is both received, and miracles are manifest through the Spirit, because of their faith.

Did Paul teach cessationism?

We've mentioned cessationism at various points in this book. Whilst this book isn't a polemic against cessationism, it is important to show where and when the New Testament corrects the notion that the gifts of the Holy Spirit were restricted to the ministry of the apostles. D.A. Carson notes that evangelical cessationism traces its roots back to B.B. Warfield:

> Who argued that signs and wonders were tied in the Bible to the purpose of attesting those of God's servants who exercised peculiar ministries in the sweep of redemptive history. Since all the public redemptive acts are behind us (except for the second advent), we should beware of counterfeit miracles in our day.[35]

However, Carson also admits that the New Testament does not support Warfield's claim that miracles were restricted to the apostles.

> There are passages that speak of gifts of healing (such as the crucial discussion of the charismata in 1 Cor 12-14) or that casually assume that more miracles were taking place among first century believers than those performed by the apostolic band and a few others (e.g., Gal 3:5 and James 5:13-16). These, I think, serve as the death knell to the strong form of the Warfield thesis. There is no sufficient evidence for supposing

---

[35] D.A. Carson, *The Purpose of Signs and Wonders in the New Testament*, a chapter in 'Power Religion: The Selling Out of The Evangelical Churches? Editor: Michael Scott Horton, p89.

that all genuine miracles came to an end at the close of the apostolic age.[36]

Carson's position is reflective of most contemporary evangelicals. There is an acknowledgement that the old cessationism, as taught by conservative evangelicals, does not do justice to New Testament account. However, it doesn't go far enough. Not only is there "no sufficient evidence" for the claim that miracles have ceased, and not only does the New Testament passages on the charismata serve as the death knell to cessationism, but the fact is also that the New Testament is *positively charismatic*. While a reluctant acknowledgement that cessationism is not really biblical, is now the majority position within evangelicalism, this position does not reflect the charismatic experience of the believers within Paul's churches. Gordon Fee expresses this point well. He argues that "Gal 3:5, (along with 1 Cor 14, 1 Thess 5:19-22 and 2 Thess 2:2) serves as further evidence of the genuinely "charismatic" nature of the Pauline churches."

1 Corinthians and Spiritual Gifts

1 Cor 12-14 are the lengthiest sections in the New Testament that deal with the gifts of the Holy Spirit. In chapter 12, Paul introduces the concept of the church as the body of Christ,

---

[36] D.A. Carson, *The Purpose of Signs and Wonders* p104.

and individual members, and their gifts being like the various parts of the body. In chapter 12, Paul bridges the overview in chapter 12, and the close up view of the gift of tongues and prophecy in chapter 14, with a section on love. In this chapter, Paul outlines the foundational Christian ethic: love. Without love, the gifts of the Holy Spirit lose their value. Without love, the gifts become an expression of selfishness rather than expressions of grace. The early Pentecostals understood this. William J. Seymour, the catalyst of Pentecostalism, said:

> The Pentecostal power, when you sum it all up, is just more of God's love. If it does not bring more of God's love, it is simply a counterfeit...Pentecost makes us love Jesus more and love our brothers more. It brings us all into one common family.

Throughout chapters 12-14 Paul is correcting, as he has been throughout the letter, several imbalances, and excesses. One of these excesses seems to have been a degree of disorder and misuse of the gifts of the Holy Spirit. Some commentators have taken Paul's rebukes to be a denial of the gifts of the Holy Spirit, however that is an obvious misinterpretation of the passages. Paul is not condemning the gifts; he is helping them steward the true gifts of the Spirit more wisely by integrating the gifts with a biblical Christology and ecclesiology. The gifts must be used to honour Christ and build up the body of Christ.

Charismatic Gifts of the Holy Spirit

In 1 Cor 12:4-12, Paul lists nine gifts of the Holy Spirit. (We know this is not an exhaustive list of God's gifts because other New Testament texts include others.)

4There are diversities of gifts, but the same Spirit.

5 There are differences of ministries, but the same Lord.

6 And there are diversities of activities, but it is the same God who works all in all.

7 But the manifestation of the Spirit is given to each one for the profit *of all*:

8 for to one is given the word of wisdom through the Spirit, to another the word of knowledge through the same Spirit,

9 to another faith by the same Spirit, to another gifts of healings by the same Spirit,

10 to another the working of miracles, to another prophecy, to another discerning of spirits, to another *different* kinds of tongues, to another the interpretation of tongues.

11 But one and the same Spirit works all these things, distributing to each one individually as He wills.

12 For as the body is one and has many members, but all the members of that one body, being many, are one body, so also *is* Christ. (1 Cor. 12:4-12 NKJ)

Let's look briefly at the various gifts that Paul mentions.

93

The Word of Wisdom

Wisdom is something that all Christians can receive. As a Christian reads and obeys scripture, spends time in prayer, and is led by the Spirit, the Christian will grow in wisdom. The manifestation of *the word of wisdom*, on the other hand, is something that the Spirit imparts as a spiritual gift. This is the ability to know what needs to be done in a particular context. The Word of wisdom was manifest during the assembly of the churches in Acts 15 where the church was unsure how to handle the gentile incorporation into the people of God.

The Word of Knowledge

Like the word of wisdom, *the word of knowledge* is supernatural knowledge that is imparted by the Spirit. It may come to a preacher as he is preaching. Revelation about a text that he has never seen before is suddenly imparted into his spirit. That is one kind of knowledge. Of course, the Spirit will never reveal knowledge that contradicts what has already been revealed in scripture. There are other kinds of knowledge that can be revealed too. The Spirit may reveal information about a person's life. We see this in John 4. Jesus operated in this gift when he conversed with the woman at the well. The purpose of this gift is always to draw people to repentance and faith in Christ.

Faith

Again, every believer has faith, and all faith is a gift, but there is a difference between the gift of faith and the measure of faith (Rom 12:3) that all Christians have. The gift of faith is the ability to trust God for the impossible. When we are faced with impossible situations, the gift of faith is something that a Christian can receive to meet the situation with utter confidence in God.

Gifts of Healings

Healing was a major part of Jesus' ministry, it was a huge part of the ministry of the church in Acts, and it should be an important part of the church's ministry today. In order to meet this need, the Holy Spirit gives gifts of healings to his people. Those who have this gift are able to pray for people, lay hands on people and see powerful results.

The Working of Miracles

Miracles followed Jesus, the apostles, and are part of the signs that accompany the preaching of the gospel and the ministry of the Holy Spirit. We explored this aspect of the ministry of the Holy Spirit when we reflected on the work of the Spirit in Galatians: "So, again I ask, does God give you his Spirit and work miracles among you by the works of the law, or by your believing what you heard?" (Gal. 3:5 NIV) Miracles are a manifestation of the Holy Spirit.

Prophecy

Prophecy is one of the most common manifestations of the Holy Spirit. For this reason, Paul spends a lot of time teaching on the details of the prophetic ministry in 1 Cor 14. We will look at those verses in the next chapter. For now it is enough to say that prophecy is Spirit-inspired speech. When it comes to prophecy, people often focus on fore-telling, they think prophecy is all about predicting future events. Fore-telling is only one aspect of prophecy, the major feature of prophecy is *forth*-telling. In other words, to speak forth the mind and will of God.

Further, it is important to note that there is a difference between the ministry gift of the prophet (Eph 4), and the gift of prophecy. All Spirit-baptised Christians can prophesy, not all who prophesy are prophets. In the same way that all Christians are called to evangelise, but not all are evangelists, so all Christians can exercise the gift of prophecy. This is what Joel prophesied when he predicted the outpouring of the Holy Spirit that would take place on the day of Pentecost.

"But this is what was spoken by the prophet Joel:

17 `And it shall come to pass in the last days, says God, That I will pour out of My Spirit on all flesh; Your sons and your daughters shall prophesy, Your young men shall see visions, Your old men shall dream dreams.

18 And on My menservants and on My maidservants I will pour out My Spirit in those days; And they shall prophesy. (Acts 2:16-18 NKJ)

In other words, the new era of the Spirit would be marked by the people of God prophesying. This would not be surprising for first century Jewish people. In the Old Testament there was a correlation between the Spirit coming upon a person, and the person prophesying. Prophecy was a common manifestation of the Holy Spirit. The New Testament teaches this too.

The apostle John records: "…your brethren who have the testimony of Jesus…For the testimony of Jesus is the spirit of prophecy." (Rev. 19:10 NKJ) Christians have the testimony of Jesus. It is the primary evidence that a person is born again. We need the Holy Spirit to profess that Jesus is Lord. However, this testimony of Jesus is also the spirit of prophecy. In other words, New Covenant believers are a prophetic people. Prophecy is not a gift for super-saints, it is for all God's people.

Discerning of spirits

When a person acts, or speaks, there can be three different spirits at work: the human spirit, the Holy Spirit or an unclean spirit. This gift enables a believer to discern the spirit that is at work. The church should be led by the Holy Spirit, but very often human spirits dominate a church's culture and direction. Likewise, sometimes demonic spirits can seek to influence a church. This gift of discernment helps us identify the source that is at work. Along with this gift, believers should cultivate spiritual authority. We are not just called to identify demons, we are called to cast them out.

Different kinds of Tongues

We now come to tongues or languages. This is by far the most misunderstood of all of the manifestations of the Holy Spirit. Firstly, it is important to note that Paul speaks of different kinds of tongues. The Greek says: "ἑτέρῳ γένη γλωσσῶν" (1 Cor. 12:10 BGT) The literal phrase is "different kinds of languages." Part of the confusion surrounding tongues is that people don't understand that there are different kinds, and different functions for tongues. Again, Paul goes into this in more detail, and we will look at that in the next chapter, but for now, it's important to note that Paul recognised the diverse and plural nature of tongues which are a manifestation of the one Holy Spirit. For example, the manifestation of tongues in Acts 2 is not the same kind of tongue that we see in the other two occasions in Acts, and they are certainly not the same kind of tongues that Paul teaches on in 1 Cor 14. In Acts 2 the tongues (or languages) were understood by the hearers, in 1 Cor 14 Paul tells us that the tongues are unintelligible mysteries that cannot be understood by the hearers unless there is a manifestation of the gift of interpretation. In Acts 2, there was no need for interpretation. Why? Whilst the tongues that were spoken were unknown to the speakers, they were understood by the bystanders who spoke those languages. This is possibly why, in 1 Cor 13, Paul mentions, "the tongues of men and *of angels.*" (1 Cor. 13:1 NKJ) In other words, sometimes the tongues we speak are earthly and can be understood by speakers of that language, and at other times they are heavenly languages that cannot be understood.

Whatever one makes of the phrase "tongues of angels" it is clear that Paul understands three different types of tongues: tongues as unlearned earthly languages (Acts 2), tongues as an unintelligible expression of thanksgiving and edification that cannot be understood naturally (1 Cor 14), and tongues which are to delivered publicly to the church, but which must be interpreted so that the church can be edified. When tongues and interpretation go together, tongues become a form of prophecy.

Paul's Pentecostal Theology

Having taken a broad overview of the ministry of the Spirit in Paul's teaching and personal experience, we will now zoom in and see how he understood the gift of tongues. We will look at his attitude towards the gift. In doing so, we will see that Paul's attitude was not critical or negative as some seem to suggest, instead Paul takes a largely positive view towards speaking in tongues.

6 Understanding Tongues

Whilst cessationism has become a minority position, and whilst there is a greater acceptance amongst evangelicals that the gifts of the Holy Spirit are for today, there is still a large amount of indifference, and veiled hostility towards the gifts of the Holy Spirit, especially the gift of tongues. Consequently, some Bible teachers filter Paul's approach to tongues through their own attitude. The outcome is that people are taught that Paul thinks tongues is a 'lesser gift' or that it really does not matter. This is not the attitude of Paul at all. It was Paul who said: 'I thank my God I speak with tongues more than you all.' (1 Cor. 14:18 NKJ) It's too easy to rush past that statement. Not only did Paul speak in tongues, but he also claimed that he used tongues more than the Corinthian believers – and they seemed to be using it a lot!

Further, Paul expressed a desire that all believers would speak in tongues: "Now I want you all to speak in tongues." (1 Cor. 14:5 ESV) Some argue that this is just Paul saying, "I wish" and that it's not directive, however, we need to remember that whilst Paul is the human author of this letter, the Holy Spirit is the ultimate author. We can then say with confidence that it is the Holy Spirit who is saying: "Now I want you all to speak in tongues." Likewise, Paul also says he desires that all believers will prophesy. He states a preference for prophecy because prophecy builds up the church, unless tongues are interpreted. The preference for tongues does not diminish the value of tongues, it just demonstrates that Paul is keen that everything that takes place builds up the body of Christ. Gordon Fee explains Paul's perspective well.

Paul is clearly not "damning tongues with faint praise," unless one argues that his positive statements are not really to be taken seriously. But quite the contrary. With interpretation even tongues becomes intelligible and is therefore one of the "greater gifts" in church. Hence the regulations on order in 14:27-28, so that tongues might become intelligible and therefore edify. That Paul values tongues as a private gift is reflected in several ways, and not simply in his "I would like every one of you to speak in tongues" (14:5) and "I thank God I speak in tongues more than all of you" (14:18).[37]

Speaking in Tongues: Irrational Babble?

One of the leading critics of the charismatic movement is John MacArthur. A few years ago, John led a conference called Strange Fire. The conference was a polemic against charismatic Christianity. John MacArthur is a great Bible teacher. Most of the time he expounds scripture powerfully. MacArthur is also correct in a lot of the excesses and abuses that he identifies within the charismatic movement. However, MacArthur makes the common mistake of being correct in what he affirms, but wrong in what he denies. He is right to identify the abuses; he is wrong in rejecting the gifts of the Spirit. Further, MacArthur's hostility towards the gifts obscures his objectivity when it comes to exegeting the biblical text. For example, MacArthur claims:

> The book of Acts depicts the gift of tongues as producing real human languages (Acts 2:9–11), and nothing in 1 Corinthians redefines tongues as irrational babble.

Of course, "irrational babble" is intentional word-choice on MacArthur's part to strike a negative tone. But let's examine the criticism. There is a difference between

---

[37] Gordon Fee, http://www.osuxa.com/wp-content/uploads/2014/07/Fee-Tongues.pdf?fbclid=IwAR2Qn3nkjoxT-NFMx7Vy2TXkorFMHAXlFRU5gwO-u7qKvJPpcONqDyKSJ9l

irrational and supra-rational. If "rational" is all about logic, and reasoning, then Paul does in fact claim that tongues bypasses the rationality of the mind. Further, if 'babble' means unintelligible, again Paul makes it clear that there is a form of tongues that is unintelligible. Paul says: "For one who speaks in a tongue speaks not to men but to God; for no one understands him, but he utters mysteries in the Spirit." (1 Cor. 14:2 ESV) Paul is clearly not describing a language that can be understood by the native speakers of that language. What is being spoken here, can be understood by no one. It is the utterance of spiritual mysteries. It is a communication between the spirit of the person praying and God. Of course, all language that is not understood by a hearer sounds like babble to the hearer. However, 'babble' can be derogatory term. If we were to write off a speaker of a foreign language because we think they are babbling, we would be regarded xenophobic and ignorant. Just because we don't understand what someone is praying when they speak in tongues, does not mean it is nonsense. There is a degree of irreverence in this criticism. Regarding mockery of tongues, Ervin writes:

> One wonders at the presumption that would arrogate to itself the right to make disparaging value judgements upon the workings of God's own Spirit. In the final analysis, only God

himself can pass judgement on his own workings.[38]

MacArthur's claim that 1 Cor 14 does not teach that there is a form of speaking in tongues that is supra-rational (again his use of 'irrational' is emotive and disingenuous) is just not the case. Paul says: "For if I pray in a tongue, my spirit prays but my mind is unfruitful. (1 Cor. 14:14 ESV) Here we have a clear teaching that praying in tongues is an activity, not of the mind, but of the spirit. This is hard for many western Christians who exalt the rational over the mystical. However, Christianity is not a western construct. There are elements of our faith that supersede rationality. Many critics don't understand how an activity that is not logical or rational can be edifying, but that does not change the fact that Paul says we can be edified by the practice of praying in tongues. Fee writes:

> The one who speaks in tongues is speaking to God (14:2) and thereby edifying himself (14:4). Such a person prays and sings with his spirit. Even if the mind is unfruitful, the clear implication is that not all Spirit-communicated edification must pass through the cortex of the brain. Such affirmations are scarcely consonant with seeing tongues as the least of the gifts.[39]

So far we have seen that there are different kind of

---

[38] Howard M. Mervin, *Spirit Baptism.*
[39] Fee.

tongues, and that one form of tongues is a heavenly language, that is both unintelligible but useful for edification. We have also been told that the one praying in tongues is speaking to God, but what kind of communication is going on?

Tongues as a form of Thanksgiving

One aspect of tongues is thanksgiving. Paul says to the one speaking in tongues: "You are giving thanks well enough." (1 Cor. 14:17 NIV) Whilst this is couched in the context of speaking in tongues not edifying others because they cannot understand, this detail that Paul gives us clarifies something of the nature of the communication that is taking place when we pray in tongues. When we praise and give thanks to God in our own languages, we ourselves are blessed and encouraged. Speaking in tongues is a form of Spirit-inspired thanksgiving. The difference between thanksgiving in tongues, and thanksgiving in our own natural language is that tongues flow directly from our spirits. The mind is not involved.

Tongues as Intercession

In Romans 8, Paul speaks of an experience of intercession in connection with the Holy Spirit that shares some of the characteristics of what he describes in 1 Cor 14.

> Likewise the Spirit helps us in our weakness. For we do not know what to pray for as we ought, but the Spirit himself intercedes for us with groanings too deep for words. (Rom. 8:26 ESV)

Fee compares this kind of praying with the praying in the spirit that Paul describes in 1 Cor 14. He argues that this interpretation, "seems to make good sense both of the present text and of the larger context of Pauline spirituality."[40]

With this in mind, we can see that tongues can manifest as either praise or intercession. This would reflect many believers' experience of praying in tongues. There are times when it can be a tremendously uplifting experience that is like jubilation and thanksgiving. At times like these our tongues can be intermingled with praise in our native tongue. On other occasions praying in tongues can come with a deep and intense burden and can be intermingled with intercession in our own natural tongues.

Tongues as Prophecy

Paul clearly discourages anyone addressing the church in tongues without interpretation. On its own, without

---

[40] Fee, *God's Empowering*, p584.

interpretation, no one can understand tongues. However, Paul argues that tongues can benefit the wider church when they are interpreted. Paul writes:

Therefore, one who speaks in a tongue should pray that he may interpret. (1 Cor. 14:13 ESV)

If any speak in a tongue, let there be only two or at most three, and each in turn, and let someone interpret. (1 Cor. 14:27 ESV)

When this happens, tongues alongside interpretation, becomes prophetic.

Various Kinds and Functions of Tongues

The various kinds of tongues, along with the various functions should cause us to be cautious about making rash judgements about how tongues functions in a local church. Many early Pentecostal leaders made distinction between tongues as 'signs following' the baptism, tongues as prayer, and tongues and interpretation as a form of prophetic ministry to the church. Further, there are many recorded testimonies of 'tongues as a sign' being understood by hearers in their own language, even though the one speaking in tongues did not speak that language. In other words, the tongues manifested in the same way that it did in Acts 2.

In the book of Acts, when tongues manifests, we see that

all who received the baptism in the Holy Spirit spoke with tongues. This is understood by many classical Pentecostals as the *sign* of tongues. This sign can either be in an earthly language (Acts 2) or an unintelligible language (Acts 10, 19). In Acts 2, the tongues were understood by the hearers (not the speakers) and in the other accounts there is no mention that anyone could understand the tongues. From this perspective we can assume that the tongues in the other accounts were the tongues that Paul describes in 1 Cor 14.

Many Pentecostals understand the *gift* of tongues to be something different to both the sign of the baptism of the Spirit and praying in tongues. As a *gift* of the Spirit, a word in tongues is addressed to a congregation and needs to be interpreted. When Paul asks: "Do all speak with tongues? Do all interpret?" (1 Cor. 12:30 ESV) the clear answer is "no." So how do we reconcile that with the claim that tongues is the sign of the baptism with the Holy Spirit? Classical Pentecostals consider the latter to be a reference to the *gift* of tongues. As said earlier, all Christians should engage in evangelism, but not all have the gift of the evangelist, all Christians can prophesy, but not all Christians are prophets and likewise, all Christians can receive tongues as a prayer language, but not all Christians have the gift of tongues to bring a message to the church.

Considering these distinctions, some Pentecostal and Charismatic groups allow for public praying in tongues as part of a prayer meeting. In this context the congregation is not being addressed directly through tongues, instead God is being addressed in a collective act of prayer and intercession. In these contexts, it is not unusual for singing in tongues to also occur. Paul says: "What am I to do? I will pray with my spirit, but I will pray with my mind also; I will sing praise with my spirit, but I will sing with my mind also." (1 Cor. 14:15 ESV) Prior to this verse, Paul has already explained that to pray in tongues is to pray with the 'spirit'. Praying with the mind is to pray with your natural language which automatically means to pray with understanding. However, he also speaks about singing in the spirit, or singing with tongues.

I have been part of services where the congregation began to sing in tongues. It is one of the most beautiful and enriching worship experiences I have ever had. It is beautiful to listen to, and it is enriching to participate in. I recall one time in a church when a wave of congregational singing in tongues swept over the meeting. I was a new Christian, I was new to speaking in tongues, but as I joined in by singing in the spirit, it seemed as if we were transported to the heavenlies. It felt as if we were caught up before the throne of grace, and joined by angels, all of us worshipping together in unity!

Non-charismatics are quick to judge congregational praying in tongues as a violation of the scriptural pattern. A number of Pentecostals and charismatics would agree, and in those contexts the only expression of tongues permitted are tongues that will be interpreted. Others, on the basis of the distinction between the *gift* of tongues, and tongues as prayer, will allow collective praying in tongues during part of the service. Where this occurs, it is generally not understood to be a violation of Paul's instructions, it is instead understood to be a form of collective praise or intercession. It must be remembered that the situations in Acts all show situations where there are collective manifestations of tongues and there are no interpreters. Further, when this happens, tongues can actually function as a sign to unbelievers: 'Thus tongues are a sign not for believers but for unbelievers' (1 Cor. 14:22 ESV). We see this in Acts 2: "we hear them telling in our own tongues the mighty works of God." And all were amazed and perplexed, saying to one another, "What does this mean?" (Acts 2:11-12 ESV) The collective expression of tongues in Acts 2 causes some to mock, and others to be stunned because of the sign of tongues. It has a converting influence on some, whereas it causes others to mock. It is no different today. I know many who encountered tongues in a worship meeting and the power of it led to their conversion.

Further Thoughts on the *Gift* of Tongues

To those who have not experienced the tongues in either collective worship or their own life, it might be difficult to grasp the distinction between the various kinds of tongues. However, this distinction is something that I have experienced. As a young believer, I heard others deliver a word in tongues (use the gift of tongues) and later the gift began to manifest in my own life.

As a new believer, I began to attend a local AoG church. Collective praying and singing in tongues were a normal part of worship. I recall when I first heard someone deliver a word in tongues. It was something very different to praying in tongues. Praying in tongues would happen all over the service. Sometimes it was an individual. Other times it was several people together. However, when a word in tongues was delivered, it felt different. There was an authority that came with it. It was not just volume, it was power. In these instances, there would *always* be an interpretation.

I recall one time I was in an independent charismatic church service and I was praying in tongues along with the congregation. Suddenly one of the leaders approached me and she said: "Keep going, that is a word in tongues." I was stunned. I did not know. I did as she asked and continued to speak out in tongues. The whole congregation quietened off when this was happening. What happened next stunned me even more. She said: "Now give the interpretation." I had never done that. I had no idea how to interpret! Suddenly the words came my mind: "Awake! Awake Zion!" I spoke that out, and then more words, in English, flowed out. I can't remember the rest of it, but it was along the lines of the Lord renewing his people and calling them closer to himself. That was the first, but not the last time I moved in this gift.

I recall a few other occasions; one was when I visited Struthers in Greenock. If anyone knows Struthers, they will know that collective praying in tongues is normal there. Again, as I was pushing into the Spirit through praying in tongues, amongst a room of about 50 others who were doing the same thing, suddenly I became aware of a shift in my tongues. The room felt it too and they quietened off. I was bringing a word in tongues. Thankfully, someone else interpreted this time! This happened on several other occasions and each time I was caught off guard by the shift in my tongues. I didn't understand how to identify the different *kind* of tongue.

Around the year 2013, I sensed the Lord leading me into a more historic reformed context. During this season I focused on the gospel and Bible teaching. The gifts of the Spirit were largely shelved. There was even a period where I questioned their validity. During that time, I stopped praying in tongues, which was a big thing for me because it was a major part of my devotional life.

Around seven years later, I was visiting an Elim church. My wife had been asked to help with the worship. There was a visiting African American prophetess speaking that night. Before the meeting she got a hold of me, prophesied over me, laid hands on me and I crashed to the floor. My kids were there, and they had grown up in a traditional Presbyterian context. My youngest said: 'Mum that woman just broke dad!'

Later that night, during the meeting, I brought a word in tongues. Just like the first time I received the gift, the prophetess turned and told me to interpret. Later that night she called both my wife and I out to the front and prophesied over us. Something changed that night. The gifts of the Spirit, particularly tongues, interpretation, and prophecy, were reactivated in my life. Almost every meeting I visited, during the worship, I could bring a word in tongues. This time, however, I could sense the gift resting on me before I brought it. I can now recognise when there is an anointing, or an unction to bring a word in tongues. I can also step into the interpretation without effort.

> Therefore, one who speaks in a tongue should pray that he may interpret. (1 Cor. 14:13 ESV)

One of the factors that is often misunderstood within evangelicalism is the assumption that we can learn all there is about the gifts from study alone. We cannot fully learn about the gifts of the Spirit from a book. The gifts need to be nurtured in real life situations. The community of believers is the context in which a person grows and develops the life of the Spirit and his gifts. The Bible helps us understand our experiences, it gives us a biblical framework and a point of reference for what we encounter spiritually. If we are to really understand the life and power which flows from speaking in tongues, we need to receive the gift and exercise it.

7 Seeking and Stirring up the Gifts

Acommon misunderstanding about the baptism in the Holy Spirit, the sign of tongues, and the other gifts of the Holy Spirit is the notion that if a person hasn't had a particular experience or if they haven't spoken in tongues, then God hasn't given them the gift and he doesn't want them to have the gift. Another way this is expressed is to say, "God is sovereign, if he wanted me to speak in tongues, he would have enabled me to do so." This kind of thinking is widespread, but it is not scriptural. What is it Paul says? "Pursue love, and earnestly desire the spiritual gifts, especially that you may prophesy." (1 Cor. 14:1 ESV) That's pretty clear. Folks interpret Paul's correction of tongues and emphasis on love to be a command to seek love and ignore tongues and the other gifts. That is not what Paul says. Paul says seek love, and *earnestly desire* the gifts – especially the gift of prophecy. Howard M. Ervin deals with this widespread misconception effectively.

> Divine initiative always courts a human response. Nonetheless, the assumption is often made that the Christian is not to seek the manifestations of the Spirit. It is frequently phrased something like this: "If God wants me to have them, He will give them to me." On the surface, this affirmation sounds convincingly pious. Actually, it is merely platitudinous. There is a rather obvious error in the tacit assumption that grace operates irresistibly upon the passive, indifferent child of God. The ancient Psalmist knew nothing of such pious self-deception when he sang: "As the heart panteth after the water brooks, so panteth my soul after thee Oh God."[41]

Ervin is using strong language, but it is needed. If we dress our apathy up as piety we need a rebuke from the Holy Spirit. If our attitude to the gifts, springs from our lack of experience of the gifts, we are not drawing our principles from the scriptures.

Preparing for Pentecost

Folk often think of the Pentecostal and Charismatic

---

[41] Ervin, *Spirit*, p132.

movements as a spontaneous outbreak of spiritual gifts. What is often forgotten is that before there was an outbreak of signs and wonders and gifts, there was hunger. Prior to the initial outpouring in Kansas with Charles Fox Parham, his students spent a period of time praying, studying the scriptures, and seeking the baptism in the Spirit with signs. It was the same with William J Seymour. Before the big meetings that drew thousands from around the globe to Azusa Street, there was the seeking and crying out at North Bonnie Brae Street. It was the same in the book of Acts, before the power of Pentecost, there was praying and pursuit of God's presence in the Upper Room. The Charismatic movement was no different. Folk were hungry for the things of the Spirit before there was a widespread move of the Spirit.

If we look to the testimonies from Azusa Street, we see that this intense hunger and "earnestly desiring the spiritual gifts" are as much a characteristic of the revival as the actual manifestations of the gifts were. Here are some examples from the revival that were printed in the Apostolic Faith which was a newspaper publication sent out by the leaders of the revival.[42]

---

[42] For those interested in these accounts, see 'When the Fire Fell: Firsthand accounts of the Azusa Street Revival' Vol 1 and 2.

EVANGELIST T.W. McCONNELL'S TESTIMONY.

About 28 years ago, I went into a meeting to break it up, and the Lord broke me up. My conversion I never could doubt. I was called to preach and refused, and went on for a number of years trying to get away from the call. Finally I obeyed the Lord, and started in to work for Him, but not to preach. The Lord sanctified my soul. Then I commenced to try to preach. About two years after, the Lord appeared to me in a dream. He so filled me with His Spirit that people were not able to stand up before me, for a time. A few days after, He told me to give up my business, and make my wants known to Him, and not to man. I obeyed. The Lord supplied my every need, and was with me in revival meetings and in healing many that I prayed for. But I heard of people receiving the Holy Ghost and speaking with tongues. I came to Los Angeles to investigate, and found it was a fact, and earnestly commenced to seek the Lord for the baptism with the Holy Ghost. And the Lord, knowing my heart, came and took possession of me and spoke with my tongue. I want to say to every person, test God and you will never deny the baptism with the Holy Ghost.[43]

Notice the humility and earnest hunger for God in this testimony. This believer could easily have responded differently to the news of the Azusa Street revival. He had already experienced the filling of the Spirit to a degree, he

---

[43] Azusa Papers.

119

had even known supernatural dreams. The Lord was using him in healing. Yet he was humble and hungry enough to seek fullness when he heard there was more. How many of us would be too proud to seek more? How many of us have lost our hunger? I am persuaded that a lack of power or gifts is not our primary problem, our primary problem is apathy and indifference to God's presence, power, and gifts. We are not thirsty enough. Here is another account of the kind of hunger that the Azusa Street revival sparked in others.

PRAYING FOR THE HOLY GHOST.

We are now hearing from individuals, and companies who are definitely waiting on God for their personal Pentecost. Some have been stimulated in seeking by hearing of God's visitation in Los Angeles. We join hands with all such hungry seekers and meet you at the throne. Some are expecting to come this way. We expect the Lord to speedily prepare such to go out into the field. Calls are coming from every direction for workers who are filled with the Spirit and have the Bible evidence. We are expecting the Lord to send out workers all over the country carrying this Gospel.[44]

So begin to pray right away for a revival in your neighbourhood or town or city. Perhaps you need one in your own closet or at your family altar first. But expect great things

---

[44] *'When the Fire Fell: Firsthand accounts of the Azusa Street Revival' Vol 1 and 2.*

from God. Begin to prepare for a revival and a great and deep revival, too, and believe for it. It may cost you money and it may cost you humbling processes, but prepare for the Lord's coming.[45]

These accounts are helpful because they not only help us get a glimpse of the power that was manifest, but they also help us to see the hunger these Christians had. Notice the call to *expect, believe and prepare*. This is the groundwork. Pentecost is not an app that can be downloaded with a quick thumb action. Pentecost comes at a price and that price is an intense longing, hungering and thirsting for the presence and power of God. Don't assume that the lack of manifestations of the Holy Spirit in your life is because God hasn't given them to you, it may well be that you just haven't earnestly sought him for all that he has for you. The promise states that it is those who seek, and keep seeking, who will find. God cannot lie. If we earnestly seek, we will experience the reality of Pentecost.

God is at work in our delays. We live in a generation of instant gratification. We have access to so much at the tip of our fingers. Almost everything is a click away. Yet God is a God of delays. Like the lover in Song of Songs, he delights in

---

[45] *'When the Fire Fell: Firsthand accounts of the Azusa Street Revival' Vol 1 and 2.*

being sought by his Bride. Very often God deals with us in the waiting process. As we seek him with our whole hearts, the Lord begins to break down issues that have been hidden in our hearts. The seeking period is a period of deep spiritual surgery. The following testimony from G.A. Cook illustrates this point well. Cook describes his period of seeking the Lord for the baptism in the Holy Spirit and the sign of tongues.

RECEIVING THE HOLY GHOST.

God has told His children to be witnesses, and the most convincing evidence is testimony of personal knowledge. To endeavour to help those who are sending in letters of inquiry to the Apostolic Faith office, asking how they may receive the Holy Ghost, the writer will state a little of his personal experience in obtaining this pearl of great price, the baptism with the Holy Ghost.

I dropped into the meetings on Azusa Street sometime in April, having heard that some people were speaking in tongues, as they did on the day of Pentecost. Although I had been trying to preach Pentecost for five years, the speaking in tongues was as strange to me as though it had never been mentioned in God's word. At first the meeting seemed a very tame affair to me, as I had been along the line of much fleshly demonstration and noise. As I was indoctrinated in the second blessing being the baptism with the Holy Ghost, I branded the teaching as heretical, not going to the meetings for some time.

In the meantime, Pentecost came to the place, and many began to speak in tongues. I now began to attend regularly. In fact, I could not stay away. My heart began to break up, and soon I was going from one person to another, asking them to forgive me for harsh words and criticism. God so melted my heart that I would cry at my work or riding on a streetcar. How the dear Lord began to teach me that what I needed was His loving, tender Spirit, and that power with God meant deep humility in our dealings with our fellow creatures.

I now began to go to the altar and earnestly seek for the Lord to have His way with me. Soon the power of God began to work with me. The Holy Ghost showed me that I must be clay in the Potter's hands, an empty vessel before the Lord. I laid aside all doctrine, all pre-conceived ideas and teachings and became absolutely empty. The Holy Ghost now settled down on me, and I could feel the power going through me like electric needles. The Spirit taught me that I must not resist the power but give way and become limp as a piece of cloth. When I did this, I fell under the power, and God began to mould me and teach me what it meant to be really surrendered to Him. I was laid out under the power five times before Pentecost really came. Each time I would come out from under the power, I would feel so sweet and clean, as though I had been run through a washing machine.

I now had come to the place where I was completely submitted to the whole will of God. I had been seeking about five weeks, and on a Saturday morning I awoke and stretched my arms toward heaven and asked God to fill me with the Holy Ghost. My arms began to tremble, and soon I was shaken violently by a great power, and it seemed as though a large pipe was fitted over my neck, my head apparently being off. I was now filled with the Holy Ghost. Words cannot describe the power I felt. The nearest description that could be given would be the action of a pump under terrific pressure, filling me with oil. I could feel the filling in my toes and all parts of my body which seemed to me to swell until I thought I would burst. I do not know how long this continued but it seemed to me a long time. The pressure was now removed and my soul and spirit seemed to leave the body and float in the air just above. My body seemed hard and metallic like iron. This was undoubtedly the baptism into the death of Christ.

It was now time for me to arise and go to work, so I got up without speaking in tongues. I believe I would have spoken in tongues then, if I had remained in the hands of the Lord long enough. About thirty hours afterwards, while sitting in the meeting on Azusa Street, I felt my throat and tongue begin to move, without any effort on my part. Soon I began to stutter and then out came a distinct language which I could hardly restrain. I talked and laughed with joy far into the night. Praise His name for such a wonderful experience of power and love and joy.

G.A. Cook.[46]

Tarrying

In relation to hungering and seeking the fullness of God and the gifts he has promised, it is no coincidence that the early Pentecostal movement became known for its 'Tarrying Meetings'. This concept seems to have emerged organically and has its roots in Jesus' instruction to the original apostles and disciples. Prior to his ascension, Jesus said: "but tarry ye in the city of Jerusalem, until ye be endued with power from on high." (Lk. 24:49 KJV) The word "tarry" means to wait. The disciples spent their time waiting, seeking, praying and expecting the gift from the Father that Jesus had promised. The early Pentecostals developed this practice of holding meetings where those seeking the baptism in the Spirit could wait and seek prayerfully.

It needs to be said that there was an important context to Jesus' original command. The Holy Spirit had not yet been poured out. There was a question of historical timing. Once the Holy Spirit was poured out at Pentecost, we do not see believers having to wait in Jerusalem until they receive the

---

[46] *'When the Fire Fell: Firsthand accounts of the Azusa Street Revival' Vol 1 and 2.*

Spirit. Although there were delays for people receiving, the delay was not because God had not yet poured out the Spirit.

Having said that, there was clearly something significant, and deeply spiritual about these early Pentecostal Tarrying Meetings. The Azusa Street newspaper gives us an insight into how widespread they were.

Mrs. C. A. Roll of 1005 Edwards Street, Ft. Worth, writes "Three of us women began to tarry and pray the last of August. About three weeks from that time, Pentecost fell on our street.

--

On arriving in the city, we were not long in finding my old friend and brother, Geo. Reilly, who was earnestly tarrying for the Pentecost. We appointed a meeting at his house the same night and he was gloriously baptized with the Holy Ghost and spoke with tongues.

--

Companies of Christians in many places are waiting on God, and tarrying for the baptism with the Holy Ghost. The most spiritual people in this land and across the ocean, and missionaries in foreign lands are writing that they are seeking the Pentecost. This is a significant fact. It means that the Lord is preparing His people for His soon coming."[47]

---

[47] '*When the Fire Fell: Firsthand accounts of the Azusa Street Revival' Vol 1 and 2.*

--

These are just three examples out of hundreds. Possibly thousands. The Tarrying Meeting became primary feature of the Pentecostal movement. It is for this reason that W.A.C. Rowe noted that the 'Tarrying Meeting' had become "an institution amongst Holy Ghost believers the world over."

However, what is to one generation a means of grace, can quickly become to the next generation a dead tradition. As the years rolled on, many kept the Tarrying Meeting intact, but the hunger and vibrancy were long gone. The next generation of Pentecostals would push back against a number of Pentecostal traditions – the Tarrying Meeting was one of the first to go. Kenneth Hagin writes:

> There is no suggestion that the people in the Early Church were ever taught to tarry to be filled with the Holy Ghost. And if we want to be thoroughly New Testament, we should never teach anyone to tarry for the baptism with the Holy Spirit either. … Why didn't I have to wait to receive? Because we don't have to tarry for a gift God has freely given to all who believe![48]

From a scriptural perspective, Hagin is correct. To make a law and a tradition out of Jesus' instructions to the original disciples who could not receive the Spirit until Pentecost

---

[48] Kenneth Hagin, Tongues: *Beyond the Upper Room*.

occurred is a mishandling of scripture. Technically a person does not have to 'tarry' or 'wait' in order to receive the Spirit. However, there is a possibility that Hagin, and modern Pentecostals and Charismatics, have missed something of the deeper principles that were at the heart of the Tarrying Meetings. It's not the label, or the structure, or the scripture about 'tarrying' that was the source of life in the early Pentecostal revivals, it was the time that was taken to be set apart and to wait on the Lord that led to such powerful breakthroughs. We can't rush God.

In many ways, it could be argued that Hagin's approach to the baptism in the Holy Spirit helped create a culture of microwave ministry. Everything from the Holy Spirit, tongues, healings, miracles and finances could now simply be claimed by faith. Intense seeking after God has given way to 'name it and claim it'. People no longer needed to spend any time seeking, they can just confess by faith. Colin Dye, the apostolic leader at Kensington Temple, makes a connection between the loss of 'Tarrying' and the superficial spiritual experience amongst modern Pentecostals and Charismatics.

In my younger days, the old Pentecostals used to speak about 'tarrying meetings' that were held across the land. These were times of waiting on the Lord for the baptism in the Spirit.

Sometimes these meetings would last for hours, even days, as people hungry for the Spirit got together in homes, mission halls and scout huts up and down the land. They would not go home until the Spirit had come in power among them. The recent move of the Spirit associated with Toronto has re-introduced these kinds of meetings in which large numbers of people come together to wait upon the Spirit and experience his power.

In the early days of the Pentecostal movement, as today, there were those who opposed this emphasis on 'waiting for the Spirit' saying that the Spirit had already come and there was, therefore, no further need to wait for him. Today, this frequently means 'taking by faith' the Spirit's presence and getting on with the Christian life regardless of any direct experience of the Spirit's power. And, needless to say, the resulting lack of power is often all too obvious. Waiting for the Spirit was not just for those believers in Jerusalem waiting for the Day of Pentecost. [49]

A lack of willingness to press in and wait for the fullness of the Holy Spirit is not just a modern problem. William J. Seymour speaks about this even during the revival.

Many people today are willing to tarry just so long, and then they give up and fail to receive their personal Pentecost that would measure with the Bible. The Lord Jesus says, "Ye shall be filled." He says that to the person that hungers and thirsts

---

[49] Colin Dye, *Hearts on Fire*.

after righteousness and He says they are blessed. So if there is a hunger and thirst in our souls for righteousness, we are blest of Him. Praise His dear name!

I am persuaded that one of the primary reasons that people have not received the fullness of the Spirit, and tongues is because we have not nurtured a culture of hunger and thirst for God. The contemporary church has recreated the priesthood and the altar by substituting the gifts of the Spirit, manifest through the congregation, for the professional band and the celebrity pastor. Pentecost was birthed and sustained by a humble black preacher who buried his head behind a couple of old crates, we've elevated our preachers on to stages, shone spotlights on them, and created a brand around these celebrity pastors. Is it any wonder the power and presence of God has departed? "I am the LORD; that is my name; my glory I give to no other, nor my praise to carved idols." (Isa. 42:8 ESV)

Whilst scripture does not give us an institution of Tarrying, and there is a danger of mistaking the form for the substance, the principles of the Tarrying Meeting, as listed and explained by the late Pentecostal leader W.A.C. Rowe are significant. We do not need to resurrect dead traditions, but the principles of the Tarrying Meeting are relevant for anyone who is serious about seeking God to be filled with the Spirit, or eager to receive the ability to speak in tongues. According to Rowe, Tarrying was about:

- Tarrying/Being set apart: "The disciples were to set themselves with determination of will, believing attitude of heart and readiness of spirit until the Holy Ghost fell on them."

- Waiting: "This is the poise of the soul in deep and intimate union and harmony with the Lord."

- Seeking: "Having tasted the Lord and found him good, the believer presses hard after a further knowledge and experience of God in the deeps and wonders of his magnetic nature. It should be remembered always that God Himself, and not the experience, ought to be the chief object of the seekers quest; the gift of the Holy Ghost, or any other of His gifts, should be the consequence that follows."

- Praying: "On many occasions it has been seen that the outpouring of prayer has made room for the inpouring of the Holy Spirit."

- Expecting: "A lively expectation is glorifying to God and it animates the whole being in a holy surging forward to the climax."

- Obtaining/Receiving: "As seeking believers advance along the royal highway towards the goal and prize, actuated by the elements which have been outlined, they will enter into and obtain the experience of the Holy Ghost in the way He has been promised, so that in its ultimate, the time of tarrying becomes the time of obtaining." [50]

When I was a young believer, I was taught by evangelical leaders that it was wrong for Christians to pray for the Holy Spirit. Yet not only does the book of Acts show us *believers* receiving or being filled with the Holy Spirit, but the Lord Jesus also encourages believers to push through in persistent prayer for the Holy Spirit.

So I say to you: Ask and it will be given to you; seek and you will find; knock and the door will be opened to you.

[10] For everyone who asks receives; the one who seeks finds; and to the one who knocks, the door will be opened.

[11] "Which of you fathers, if your son asks for a fish, will give him a snake instead?

[12] Or if he asks for an egg, will give him a scorpion?

[13] If you then, though you are evil, know how to give good gifts to your children, how much more will your Father in heaven give the Holy Spirit to those who ask him!" (Lk. 11:9-13 NIV)

The original Greek captures the sense of these instructions more clearly. Believers are to *keep asking, keep seeking, and keep*

[50] Rowe, One Lord, One Faith, p144-145.

knocking. This is to be an ongoing condition of the heart.

Further, notice what Jesus tells his disciples this persistent asking should be for: the Holy Spirit. We are to ask for the Holy Spirit.

Many believers, because of the controversy surrounding the gifts of the Spirit, are afraid of being deceived. They don't want to receive a counterfeit spirit. I recall in my early days another Christian telling me a story that was designed to scare young Christians away from seeking tongues. He claimed he had heard of a Satan worshipper attending a local church where believers were praying in tongues. Apparently the Satan worshipper said to the church: "Why are you all worshipping Satan? That's the language we use as devil worshippers." Of course, such a story is an urban myth. It never happened. Yet, were it true, it is ironic that many evangelicals are more ready to receive the testimony of a Satan worshipper than they are willing to hear the testimony of Spirit-filled believers who are worshipping Jesus and grateful for their new sense of spiritual life that has come through the gifts of the Spirit! However, these words of Jesus should put our fears to rest.[51] If we seek God for the Holy Spirit, he will not give us a scorpion. We need

---

[51] This is not to say that there is no such thing as counterfeit tongues. However, a holy life, a life of repentance, and a mind set on the Word of God are safeguards against these things.

to anchor our seeking of the Spirit's fullness in the goodness and love of God.

God wants us to seek him. He commands us to 'earnestly seek spiritual gifts.' There is much more available to all of us than what we have already received. Let's press in and receive all that God has for us.

You, God, are my God, earnestly I seek you; I thirst for you, my whole being longs for you, in a dry and parched land where there is no water.

2 I have seen you in the sanctuary and beheld your power and your glory. (Ps. 63:1-2 NIV)

8 Benefits of Tongues

In many ways, the various theological understandings of Spirit-baptism and tongues are a secondary issue compared with the reality of experiencing the Spirit's empowering presence and speaking in tongues. The reality is the Spirit's empowering presence is found amongst people who hold to Sacramental, Evangelical, and Pentecostal understandings of Spirit baptism. In some sense, it is less important how we label or define the reality of the Holy Spirit's gifts, it's more important that we experience the reality of it. Whether a person understands their experience of the Spirit as the baptism of the Spirit, or the empowering of the Spirit, or the filling of the Spirit, or anointing, is less important than the reality of encountering the fullness of God and his gifts.

Likewise, if a thorough study of the scriptures causes a

Christian to be persuaded that tongues is not a sign that follows the baptism in the Holy Spirit, this should not lead a person to conclude that tongues is not available to them. I would never say that every Christian *must* speak in tongues, that would be legalistic. I do however believe that every Christian has the potential to receive and exercise tongues as a prayer language. Every Christian *may* speak in tongues.

This view was held by John Wimber. Whilst Wimber did not teach baptism in the Holy Spirit as a subsequent experience, and he did not teach that tongues were the sign of the baptism in the Spirit (for Wimber, baptism in the Spirit happens at conversion) Wimber *did* teach that Christians should expect ongoing empowering of the Spirit and also that *tongues is available to every believer*. It should also be noted that Wimber's movement was a catalyst for many evangelicals discovering the reality of signs and wonders. Wimber may not have been a Pentecostal or a Charismatic, but he certainly moved in the reality of the Spirit's power, and enabled others to do the same. Regarding tongues, Wimber says this:

> One of the most often asked question is, "Are tongues for everyone?" So far in my experience, it has been. I have not seen anyone yet who wanted to speak in tongues that has not received it, although I have seen some who struggle with it.

Most who have problems come from a background which has an anti-tongues theology. They have been taught that this is not a present day gift to experience. Unlearning for these people often takes time. Scriptural opposition is usually raised from the passage in **1 Corinthians**, which asks the question, "Do all speak in tongues?" It is often pointed out that the Greek language requires a "no" as the answer.

On the surface this seems an adequate response; however the context of the whole passage must be taken into consideration. The context began with **1 Corinthians 11:17** and continues through 14:40. Without taking you through all the reasons, let me suggest that I think the key is when the body comes together. Within that frame of reference, Paul is asking the questions recorded at the end of chapter 12. When the body comes together, "Are all Apostles?" "No!" "Do all have the gifts of healing?" "No!" "Do all speak in tongues?" "No!" "Do all interpret?" "No!"

This passage does not mean that all cannot speak in tongues. It does mean that when the body of Christ gets together, all do not have to speak in tongues. There are five reasons why I believe one ought to pray in the Spirit. [Pray in tongues.]

1.   It can be a sign for unbelievers (**1 Corinthians 14:22**)

2.   It is a form of petition (**Ephesians 6:18**)

3.   It can be a time of edification for the one praying (**1 Corinthians 14:4**)

4.   It is part of our spiritual armament (**Ephesians 6:18**)

5.   It gives praise to God (**1 Corinthians 14:2**)[52]

Jack Hayford is a well-known Pentecostal pastor who, whilst coming from a different tradition to Wimber, has arrived at a similar position to him. Hayford sees tremendous results when he prays for people to receive tongues and believes that the Spirit enabled ability to pray in tongues is available to all believers who seek the gift. In his book: 'The Beauty of Spiritual Language', Hayford writes an honest account of his struggle with his denomination's teaching that tongues is the 'initial physical evidence' of the baptism in the Holy Spirit. As a result, Hayford describes how he was led to rearticulate how he taught on the gifts. I quote him at length because of the relevance of his reflections.

> Who could dare insist on an absolute requirement that tongues be an ironclad rule—a demanded sign to verify the infilling of the Holy Spirit?
>
> On the other hand, as I honestly weighed all this, I was still finding consistent results as I encouraged people to expect to speak with tongues when they asked the Lord Jesus Christ to fill them with the Holy Spirit and power. Of course, I had originally been motivated to do this for doctrinal reasons, believing tongues were mandated.

---

[52] John Wimber

But though my conviction as to a "mandate" was waning, there still seemed an apparent willingness of the Lord to respond in grace, however imperfect my view may have been. People met Jesus regularly, in a mighty way — in overflowing fullness. And even though tongues were never forced on anyone, the unthreatening atmosphere of expectation resulted in virtually all receiving a spiritual language at the same time they were filled.

Because there are at least three biblical cases of this sign being manifested in this way, I didn't feel I was operating with thin evidence. At Pentecost (Acts 2:4), at Cornelius' house (Acts 10:44–48), and at Ephesus (Acts 19:6), the sign of speaking with tongues plainly accompanies people's receiving their initial infilling of the Holy Spirit. But I still couldn't rest in the notion that God's intent in this sign was being properly understood. Was it meant as a proof? Or rather, was it meant as a provision?

I was beginning to suspect the latter was the case: that tongues had been given as a divine provision — a beneficial resource, always available where faith-without-fear was ready to receive and exercise spiritual language. The undeniable breadth revealed in the scriptures, along with the inescapable evidence throughout the Christian community, was forcing me away from my doctrinal posturing.

My first decisive steps began with what was for me the risk of appearing to compromise by deciding to admit the obvious.

There were and are too many people I know who live power-filled lives under the touch and gifts of the Holy Spirit, though they have never spoken with tongues.

I determined to cease contending for another definition of their fullness, and I refused to deny their anointed ministry as being anything other than fully Spirit-filled. But as surely as to deny that would have been dishonest, it would have been equally unwise for me to retreat from what I was discovering about tongues as a provision for all believers — for prayer and praise.

Proven results in my own ministry evidenced people almost always receiving spiritual language when they welcomed the fullness of the Spirit into their lives. I had no reason to cease teaching this expectation, but how was I to merge these two convictions I was reaching? I was convinced I couldn't demand tongues as an evidence of Holy Spirit-fullness; and I was convinced I couldn't deny the availability or value of tongues if welcomed by those seeking His fullness.[53]

Scriptural Basis for Tongues being Available to Every Believer

From my perspective, I believe the manifestation of tongues is available to every Christian for a number of reasons. Firstly, I believe this because of what Paul teaches in 1 Cor.

---

[53] Jack Hayford, *The Beauty of Spiritual Language.*

14. Paul says: "Follow the way of love and eagerly desire gifts of the Spirit, especially prophecy." (1 Cor. 14:1 NIV) Personally, I don't think enough Christians feel the weight of these commandments. We are not told to be passive about the gifts, we are not told that God will drop them upon the heads of indifferent believers, we are told to earnestly, intensely and passionately desire the gifts – and this includes tongues.

Further, Paul says: "I would like every one of you to speak in tongues." (1 Cor. 14:5 NIV) Paul's desire is that all believers operate in this gift. He isn't saying he wants them all to be able to bring a public message in tongues, he is talking about tongues as a private prayer language. This is why Paul says: "I thank God that I speak in tongues more than all of you. But in the church I would rather speak five intelligible words to instruct others than ten thousand words in a tongue." (1 Cor. 14:18-19 NIV) From this we can clearly see that Paul's attitude towards the gift is not negative. He tells them to intensely seek the gifts, he desires that they speak in tongues, and he himself says he speaks in tongues (privately) more than all of them – and they were speaking in tongues a lot!

This leads into another reason why I believe tongues, as a private prayer language, is available to all believers.

Tongues is the only gift that is given for self-edification. Paul says: "Anyone who speaks in a tongue edifies themselves." (1 Cor. 14:4 NIV) All of the other gifts are given for us to bless others, whereas praying in tongues helps the one praying to experience blessing. In other words, it is a gift that is given to enhance our devotion and personal discipleship. This is a primary reason that I believe the gift is available to all believers.

Finally, my experience of seeing and hearing how people receive the gift encourages me to believe that it is available for all. I, myself, have prayed for people to receive the gift, and they have. Others have shared with me their journey of seeking and receiving the gift. Each time, whilst there may have been a period of delay or struggle, but those who share their stories of seeking the gift also have a testimony of breakthrough.

In terms of the universality of tongues, Alistair Matheson says:

> The gift of tongues has been made available without discrimination to all Christians regardless of nationality, age, gender academic privilege, or historical context. If tongues are from God, then we should desire to see them exercised privately and in the church.[54]

---

[54] Alistair Matheson, *Highland Pentecost*, p65.

Tongues as Personal Edification

Regarding the purpose and benefits of praying in tongues, Paul says: "Anyone who speaks in a tongue edifies themselves." (1 Cor. 14:4 NIV)

In the original Greek, this word literally means: *to build* as in "constructing houses or temples." This is significant, individually, and collectively, believers are the building and the temple of God. When we pray in tongues, we are building ourselves up. We are building up the temple of the Holy Spirit. The temple is the place where God's presence dwells. As we pray in the Spirit, we will become more conscious and more yielded to the presence of God who dwells within us. We will also see greater manifestations of the presence of God through us. Ezekiel writes: "and there was water, flowing from under the threshold of the temple toward the east." (Ezek. 47:1 NKJ) When we pray in tongues, we make room for the Holy Spirit to flow through us and out of us like a river. This river will bring refreshing to those whom we come into contact with.

Figuratively, the word means to "make more able", or to "strengthen". This is also significant. Praying in tongues strengthens us and makes us more able to be used by God. Hugh Black writes the following instructions for speaking in tongues:

> Those of you who have the gift should 'stir up the gift' that is in you. In your prayer times speak much to the Lord in tongues. Go through in that realm of the Spirit until you are able to pour your burdens out in unknown languages. Sometimes when you are called to pray for a person, you will not know how to pray as you ought. You can then open your being to the moving of the Spirit, and may know the flooding of tongues coming through you effectively and gloriously. Never become light about tongues – never regard them cheaply, but come under the full control of the Holy Spirit and use them under his power. ... Give yourself to your ministry, deepen your gift, let the power of the Holy Spirit flow through you until the glory of God comes with your utterances.[55]

It is important to note that the late Hugh Black was mightily used in evangelism, healing, deliverance and leading people to receive the baptism in the Holy Spirit. I had the privilege of hearing him preach on a few occasions. When the man spoke, there was a deep sense of God's presence that seemed to accompany his words. God seemed to fill the room. Mr. Black is not giving us some abstract theory, this is a reality that he lived in and ministered in.

It's also important to note Mr. Black's comments about not treating tongues cheaply or lightly and his call for us to

---

[55] Hugh Black, Christian Fundamentals, p85.

deepen the gift. I have to confess that I have not always held the tongues with the reverence that the gifts of God should be held with. When we move into the realm of the gifts of the Spirit, we are moving into holy ground.

Further, Mr. Black reminds us we can deepen our gift, and by doing so, deepen our experience of the gift. Perhaps one of the reasons why so many of us have shelved tongues is because we have not learned to use it to push through into the depths of God. The more we pray in tongues, the more our language will develop and deepen. If we only churn out a couple of words in tongues, in church, once a week, for a couple of minutes, it is no wonder we are not mining the riches of this gift.

The riches that come from praying in tongues can ultimately only be discovered by experience. Study alone will not yield its fruits. W.A.C. Rowe says:

> One must experience the effective blessing and joyous glory of speaking in tongues to really understand and appreciate the gift. The anointed expression of it is very satisfying to the spirit of the one exercising the gift. Really, no one can fully understand or effectively discuss speaking in tongues who has not entered into the experience.[56]

---

[56] Rowe, *One*, p183.

Gateway into Other Gifts

Praying in tongues is not a stand-alone gift. When we pray in tongues we open ourselves up to being able to move in other gifts. For example, Paul says: "the one who speaks in a tongue should pray that they may interpret what they say." (1 Cor. 14:13 NIV) From this we can see that one gift can lead into another. If we are speaking in tongues, Paul says we should pray for interpretation. If you start to receive the gift of interpretation for your tongues, you are starting to move in the prophetic. Tongues, when they are interpreted, become prophecy.

Testimonies about Tongues

Whilst I was preparing this manuscript, I asked a number of friends to send me some testimonies about how the ministry of tongues had made a difference in their lives. I asked some of them to share their story about how they received the gift, and how it made a difference to their walk with God. A pastor friend wrote to me and said, "It's my honest conviction, based on scripture and my experience, that my life and ministry wouldn't be anywhere near as effective if I didn't pray in tongues every day."

Another pastor friend sent the following testimony about his experience with tongues.

It is like tongues creates a direct line to God no matter what the current spiritual climate is. Think of the matrix when Neo or others are being chased by the agent Smith. They need to talk to Zion to escape (via telephone). Not only can we praise and adore the Lord, but we can instantly hear God. Tongues are like a springboard to the other gifts. I can think of a time recently before preaching the gospel, I worshipped and prayed in tongues for about an hour, in a heavy spiritual environment. I then preached as the Spirit led me. It was boldness beyond human ability, and one of the drunks in the crowd stood up crying with his arms in air to receive the Lord. I cried out in the Spirit five times directly to another person in the crowd that he needed to be saved *now* and *believe*. The rule, reign and government of the Lord was present to give them the opportunity to repent and change their lives in that moment!

Here are some further testimonies from people who experienced tongues many years ago. In their story, each of them describes how they received the gift and the impact the gift has had upon their lives.

Graham's Story

I was 21 years old, alone in my bedroom, and praying to God as I had done since I became a Christian aged 9. Suddenly this well of anger burst out of me towards my father who had left my mum and I when I was a toddler.

Like a cork out of a bottle it exploded into shouting and tears, until I slumped on the bed exhausted, feeling so abandoned. Prompted by the Spirit I opened my Bible at Isaiah 43 as God ministered His Father love like never before. Overcome, I stood up to pray and began babbling strange words and sounds. Like a dam bursting, the river of sounds flowed, and I realised I was speaking in tongues for the first time.

In the weeks that followed, I learned that I could speak in tongues whenever I wanted, now that the gift had been given to me, I could use it for God's glory. I also thought of it as a new muscle to exercise, so I would, "do a 5k or a 10k" (speaking in tongues for 5 or 10 minutes) and even a "marathon" (26 minutes). The immediate effect was to bring me closer to God when I felt far away. I began to hear God's inner voice more clearly. I began to prophesy, and people would confirm the accuracy of the prophecies. I could discern the presence of evil and pray for people to be delivered of evil spirits. My hunger for God grew and my passion for service.

Being baptised in the Spirit at age 21 with the accompaniment of speaking in tongues was like going through a door into the spiritual realm, and one from which

I have never returned.[57]

John's Story

For over 42 years, I have practiced praying in the Spirit (tongues), and from my very first encounter of hearing Christians speaking in tongues until I was able to speak in tongues myself, it took about a year. I do not believe it should take that long if you have the right teaching when you first becoming a Christian. I became a Christian in a denomination that believed those gifts had passed away, that the days of miracles were over, so having to combat unbelief and uproot it out of my life took some time.

When I did begin to speak in tongues, I was praying with two other Christians, suddenly they began to sing in tongues, and suddenly, I felt I wanted to sing too and as I did this new language bubbled up from deep within my belly and came tumbling off my tongue without any thought or effort, it all felt very normal and natural in my ongoing Christian experience.

I believe it is vitally important for every believer to practice, as a spiritual discipline, speaking in tongues daily. I find that many who can pray in the spirit, utter a few signature words and syllables, now and again, especially at

[57] Graham is the pastor of Hope Hall Church Paisley.

the end of worship, and fail to develop speaking in tongues any further than a few words, instead of it developing into a rich language of conversation with the Father and Jesus through the Holy Spirit. The result is that they miss the importance and power that comes when praying in the Spirit, that the old Pentecostals found at the beginning of the 20th century when they would pray through for hours in the Spirit.

I find praying in tongues builds me up spiritually, it makes me sensitive to the spiritual realm and the things of the Spirit and opens the way for other gifts to manifest in the realm of the supernatural.

I have discovered that praying in the Spirit is different from the gift of tongues that needs the gift of interpretation to manifest with it. How I discovered this was that when I pray in my prayer language it sounds the same language, I cannot speak French of German but if someone speaks French or German, I know the sound of those languages. When the gift of diverse tongues begins to operate, I have found I have a sense of the presence and anointing on my soul and I know my prayer language will begin to flow in different sounds of new languages, then there needs to be an interpretation. I still believe as I pray in my prayer language that interpretations come but it's usually in the flow of prayers and praise which is upwards to God and gives me insight into things I am praying for.

I would encourage every believer to seek God for the infilling of the Holy Spirit and the sign of tongues that is supposed to follow all who are believers, and when you get it, use it as often as you can, and it will take you into a new dimension of your Christian experience and life.[58]

Janice's Story

As a young Christian, I'd been strongly advised not to venture into the book of Revelation. I knew it was different from the other books of the Bible and was I curious. "No don't I was told, it'll only confuse you." These well-meaning Christians were concerned it would somehow frighten me off my new faith. But the words, "It'll only confuse you," kept playing over in my mind. I concluded that this just couldn't be right, how can God's word confuse? So, in I went to the book of Revelation.

I didn't understand most of it but do remember how thrilled I was to arrive at Rev 1:14-20. A beautiful description of the Lord. How wonderful! I could just imagine how beautiful He is and was determined to press in.

I continued on but didn't realise I was about to trip over a massive stumbling stone. Rev 20:15. "Anyone not found

---

[58] John is a Baptist Minister, and he pastors Berwick Baptist Church.

written in the Book of Life, was to be cast into the lake of fire." Help! I remember thinking, "My name can't possibly be in there, I've not been saved long enough!" Funny now, but a sobering thought then.

I attempted to call two (the only two) Christians I knew, neither were home and this was urgent. Then a young preacher I knew came to mind. I called him, apologised for taking his time and explained the whole situation. He patiently went through the scriptures with me explaining that the minute I'd received Christ as Saviour, my sins were forgiven and my name was written in the Lamb's Book of Life. Jesus died on the cross for me, and the instant I received Him as Saviour, I was transferred from death to life. I remember the relief I felt.

The conversation continued with a life changing question, "Are you baptised in the Holy Spirit?" I didn't know what that was, but I did know if it was from the Lord then I wanted it, urgently. I replied, "No. What is that?" I can't remember all that he said, but he convinced me it was of God. "Have you heard of the gift of tongues?" he then asked. The conversation was now becoming difficult to follow.

"No, what's that?" (I didn't really want to know, I already had so much information floating around in my head, and I was more concerned about the baptism of the Holy Spirit.) He suggested I go ask the Holy Spirit.

I still have a vivid recollection, 40 years later, of what followed. I finished that call, walked to the middle of the room, and fell to my knees. I then informed the Lord of the whole conversation that had just taken place (as if he didn't know already!). I was about to ask if I could have the baptism of the Holy Spirit, I couldn't finish the question. I'd only gotten half-way through the request when something strange began to happen in my mouth. My tongue was behaving strangely, it felt weird. I remember I immediately stopped talking and began to pray silently. I told the Lord that the devil was trying to stop me talking to Him, and I would now pray silently. I was defiantly determined he was not going to stop me praying. All of a sudden, what I can only describe as a sudden rush of power, rose up from deep within me bringing with it a steely determination. I remember in an instant thinking the devil would not stop me talking to the Lord. As I opened my mouth to continue with my newfound confidence, sounds I couldn't understand came pouring out of my mouth. But I knew, it wasn't the devil, it was the Holy Spirit, and I was now speaking in a strange new language I'd never heard before. It was tongues. It was undeniable proof for me that

God was real, proof that He listens when I pray, proof that He was right here with me, proof that He loves me. I cried so hard I could not speak for two days.

My journey with my friend the Holy Spirit began that day. He has been so gracious throughout a sometimes difficult journey. He has shown me much and He's taught me much, I've not always been the best student, but I thank Him that to this day, He's never left me.[59]

Allana's Story

I was a relatively new Christian when someone told me I was a prayer warrior. I'd no idea what that meant. So, I started to read books about prayer, and I noticed writers talked about speaking in tongues when you pray. This was news to me. I went to a traditional Church of Scotland and no-one was doing this during the Sunday service.

After a while, I started to attend an evangelical church. Our fellowship was definitely encouraged to use this Holy Spirit gift at home and in church when we met together for worship and prayer. But how did you get it? And what happened once you did?

I went to the Bible and looked for scriptures which mentioned people speaking in tongues. The apostles of Jesus found themselves speaking in tongues at Pentecost,

---

[59] Janice has many years' experience in church planting and prophetic ministry.

when the Holy Spirit was poured out on them. It happened to others when believers prayed for them. So during my prayer time I'd be asking God for this spiritual gift. Several times other believers prayed the same thing for me too. Nothing happened.

Perhaps my motivation to have this particular gift was dodgy? Did I really want it to build up my spiritual life and connect with God in a deeper way? Was I sensing it might make my prayer time more powerful because the Holy Spirit would relay what my heart could barely express? Or was I seeking this gift as proof that I was a born again, spirit-filled Christian? Though scripture says not everyone speaks in tongues.

Here's the good news. Within two years I discovered that all these prayer requests had been answered. The downside is I can't pinpoint exactly when it happened. Over that time, I'd regularly hear fellow believers speak in their heavenly language. I tried to imitate these sounds in the privacy of my own home, but it didn't feel right.

I expected some kind of spontaneous flow of syllables to come out of my mouth. In the book of Acts, new converts were able to speak in tongues straight away. They didn't seem to need any practice. I assumed that fluency came with the gift.

I visited a local Christian bookshop and bought a CD on the subject. I was hoping for a step by step DIY guide. As I listened, I found myself making a few unintelligible sounds. These didn't match what I recognised at church meetings, so that was that.

Thankfully, God is very gracious to this slow learner. Soon, I went to an event held by the Full Gospel Businessmen's Fellowship. People could go forward for prayer and I did. I shared about wanting to speak in tongues and that it hadn't happened yet.

I recall this kindly man asking if I'd ever found myself making any sort of sounds as I prayed for this gift. I told him all I'd got was a few syllables. He invited me to repeat them in that noisy hall, where I almost had to shout my 'Kee-ar-ash' into his ear. He nodded, and said, 'You're doing it.' My stunned reply was 'Really? That's IT?'

He explained that speaking in tongues was a bit like riding a bike. The more I let whatever few sounds came out of my mouth, the easier it would become. He told me even more would likely follow, so just relax, carry on and go for it.

That's exactly what has happened. The benefits from being able to exercise this gift in my spiritual life are huge. When I start to use this alternative to words, I feel freer. My rational (and critical) mind has no say in how my prayers are expressed. The Holy Spirit is in charge. Speaking in tongues brings my focus onto God, it kick starts me into His presence. Worship can do that too, and I love to sing in tongues.

There are times when I'm babbling away and a scripture pops into my thoughts for a person or situation. On other occasions, the flow of sounds will quicken and grow louder, as if I'm making a declaration or doing some spiritual warfare. I can also find myself suddenly speaking in tongues and I've no idea who or what I'm praying for. Using this gift makes my faith rise, and power is being released when believers do it.

I'm no expert, but I know I wouldn't want to be without this gift. What's next on my prayer list? I'm asking for the gift of interpretation. I want revelation of what people say in tongues to inform and edify my fellow followers of Christ. Watch this space.[60]

A Common Testimony

These testimonies are incredibly encouraging. I've added them to this book for a couple of reasons. Each testimony

---

[60] Allana Dymock attends her local Elim church, and is also involved with *Light and Life*, a prophetic-missional ministry. In previous years she was also involved in Healing Rooms Scotland.

shows the diverse ways that God uses to bring people into the experience, and each story clearly signals the benefits that speaking in tongues brought to the believer. If you are reading this, and you have not yet received the gift, I hope you are encouraged by these testimonies. I hope you are encouraged to press in and receive the gift for yourself. On the other hand, if you already have the gift, but you have not been using it much, I hope these testimonies help you recall your own initial experience and the spiritual benefits you gained at the time. I hope you are encouraged to rekindle your tongues of fire.

As we pray in the Spirit, we move into a deeper communion with God. This in turn enables us to receive understanding of what we are praying in the Spirit. We should expect to see an overflow. Prophecy, words of wisdom and knowledge may also flow are a result of our ministry in tongues. Likewise, our missional boldness and sensitivity to the Spirit should also be increased. In my own life, as a new Christian, a strong evangelistic anointing flowed from time spent praying in tongues. I have also found that praying in tongues, prior to preaching enhances the sense of unction and freedom that accompanies the preaching of the gospel. In the next chapter, we will look more closely at the connection between speaking in tongues and effective mission.

9 Tongues and Missional Empowerment

In the book of Acts, there is a clear connection between the missional calling of the church and the empowering of the Spirit for mission. Jesus, before his ascension, said to the disciples: "But you will receive power when the Holy Spirit comes on you; and you will be my witnesses in Jerusalem, and in all Judea and Samaria, and to the ends of the earth." (Acts 1:8 NIV) This promise of power was received on the day of Pentecost, for we read:

All of them were filled with the Holy Spirit and began to speak in other tongues as the Spirit enabled them.

5 Now there were staying in Jerusalem God-fearing Jews from every nation under heaven.

6 When they heard this sound, a crowd came together in bewilderment, because each one heard their own language being spoken.

⁷ Utterly amazed, they asked: "Aren't all these who are speaking Galileans?

⁸ Then how is it that each of us hears them in our native language? (Acts 2:4-8 NIV)

The outpouring of the Spirit has an immediate impact upon a crowd of international Jews. Once the crowd's attention was captured, Peter, who previously denied his faith because of fear, stood up a transformed man and proclaimed the gospel under a new anointing of the Holy Spirit:

Then Peter stood up with the Eleven, raised his voice and addressed the crowd: "Fellow Jews and all of you who live in Jerusalem, let me explain this to you; listen carefully to what I say.

¹⁵ These people are not drunk, as you suppose. It's only nine in the morning!

¹⁶ No, this is what was spoken by the prophet Joel:

¹⁷ "'In the last days, God says, I will pour out my Spirit on all people. Your sons and daughters will prophesy, your young men will see visions, your old men will dream dreams. (Acts 2:14-17 NIV)

Once he gets through with his sermon, the results are cataclysmic: "Those who accepted his message were baptized, and about three thousand were added to their number that day." (Acts 2:41 NIV)

There is no less a connection between the theology and experience of Pentecostalism, and the theology and experience we encounter in Acts. The outpouring of the Spirit in Acts led to the global spread of the gospel, the outpouring of the Spirit at the turn of the twentieth century also led to a new wave of global mission. This was no coincidence, the theological founder of the movement, Charles Fox Parham, understood there was a direct connection between the baptism in the Holy Spirit, the sign of tongues, and a global harvest.

Missionary Tongues in Early Pentecostalism

It is worth noting at this point the historical reasoning behind the classical Pentecostal view that tongues are the sign of the baptism of the Holy Spirit. In Parham's thinking, tongues were always languages that could be understood (xenoglossia or xenolalia). It was believed that global missionary activity would be greatly sped up if missionaries were supernaturally empowered to proclaim the gospel to nations in a language they did not have to spend years learning. The early Pentecostal movement was full of testimonies of missionaries receiving their 'tongue' and travelling by faith to far off countries to preach the gospel in the native tongue of the people. Examples of these accounts are well documented in the Azusa Street's newsletter.

RUSSIANS HEAR IN THEIR OWN TONGUE.

Different nationalities are now hearing the Gospel in their own "tongue wherein they were born." Sister Anna Hall spoke to the Russians in their church in Los Angeles, in their own language as the Spirit gave utterance. They were so glad to hear the truth that they wept and even kissed her hands. They are a very simple, pure, and hungry people for the full Gospel. The other night, as a company of Russians were present in the meeting, Bro. Lee, a converted Catholic, was permitted to speak their language. As he spoke and sang, one of the Russians came up and embraced him. It was a holy sight, and the Spirit fell upon the Russians, as well as on others, and they glorified God.[61]

Parham's view of tongues would eventually be redefined. One of the main reasons for this was the discovery that the tongues were often not a specific language. William J. Seymour, that catalyst of the Azusa revival, had never been fully persuaded by Parham's understanding of tongues. Seymour understood tongues as unknown languages (glossolalia). It was Seymour's definition of tongues that would become the mainstream view within the Pentecostal movement. Nevertheless, testimonies of xenoglossia never

---

[61] *When the Fire Fell: Firsthand accounts of the Azusa Street Revival' Vol 1 and 2.*

vanished completely. Testimonies of xenoglossia are recorded in many early Pentecostal historical documents.

The doctrine of Spirit baptism and tongues was not the fanatical ramblings of some fringe sect that would soon die out, on the contrary, this teaching and experience has sparked the fastest growing global missional movement in the world. Current stats inform us:

By 2050, Charismatic Christians will outnumber the non-religious.

The total of all non-religious individuals around the world currently sits at more than 878 million, while Pentecostal/Charismatic Christians number 644 million.

In the next 30 years, however, that branch of Christianity will top 1 billion, while the non-religious will be closing in on 850 million.[62]

Azusa Street, we would say today, went 'viral'. And this was before the internet. Pentecostal Historian A.H. Anderson notes:

By 1910, only four years after the commencement of the Azusa Street revival, it was reported that Pentecostal missionaries from Europe and North America were in over fifty nations of the world.[63]

---

[62] 10 Encouraging Trends of Global Christianity in 2020 - Lifeway Research
[63] Anderson, *Introduction.*

The Holy Spirit and Pentecostal Missionary Work

How can the explosive growth, of what began as a fringe revival movement which held to what was regarded as strange teachings and strange tongues, be understood? Anderson connects the growth of the movement with its two-fold understanding of mission and the Holy Spirit.

One of the reasons for the rapid growth of Pentecostalism is because it has always had a strong emphasis on mission and evangelism. From the beginning, Pentecostals and Charismatics have been involved in these activities, coming from a strong Christocentric message and pneumatological focus. Indeed, the first Pentecostals believed that the Spirit had been poured out on them in order to engage in the end-time harvest of souls that would accompany the preaching of the 'full gospel' throughout the world. Their efforts were grounded in the conviction that the Holy Spirit was the motivating power behind all such activity, and their Spirit baptism had given them different languages of the world, as the first issue of the Azusa Street newspaper declared:

A minister says that God showed him twenty years ago that the divine plan for missionaries was that they might receive the gift of tongues either before going to the foreign field or on the way. It should be a sign to the heathen that the message is of God. The gift of languages can only be viewed as the Spirit gives utterance. It cannot be learned like the native tongues, but the Lord takes control of the organs of speech at will. It is emphatically, God's message.

The fact that most of the early missionaries did not speak the languages of the people to whom they went did not deter them, for they were not motivated by the tongues they had been given, but by the Spirit in them. Pentecostals place primary emphasis on being 'sent by the Spirit' and depend more on what is described as the Spirit's leading than on formal structures. People called 'missionaries' did that job because the Spirit directed them to do it, often through some revelation like a prophecy, a dream or a vision, and even through an audible voice perceived to be that of God.[64]

Anderson makes a further point regarding the role of the Spirit in Pentecostal missional activity.

In comparison to the 'Missio Dei' of older Catholic and Protestant missions and the 'obedience to the Great Commission' of evangelical missions, Pentecostal mission is grounded foremost in the conviction that the Spirit is the motivating power behind this activity. Pentecostal leader J. Roswell Flower wrote in 1908, 'When the Holy Spirit comes into our hearts, the missionary spirit comes in with it; they are inseparable … Carrying the gospel to hungry souls in this and other lands is but a natural result.' The heart of Pentecostal missions is the experience of the power of the Spirit.[65]

Despite the tremendous growth and missional impact of

---

[64] *A.H. Anderson, An Introduction to Pentecostalism.*
[65] Anderson, *Introduction.*

Pentecostalism, the movement has struggled and stagnated at various points in its history. By 1927, Pentecostal pioneer, John G. Lake was lamenting the state of the movement. Lake asks: "Are we to simply witness the dying of Pentecost as other lesser revelations of God have come to the world, fluttered and sputtered for a few years and then disappeared?"[66] However the movement experienced trouble long before this. Prior to the emerging apostolic and evangelistic ministry of George Jeffreys in 1912, E.C.W Boulton wrote: "It almost seemed as though the movement was suffering from the paralysis of passivity."[67]

Recovering Missionary Tongues

Denzil R. Miller argues that one of the reasons that Pentecostalism has lost its edge is because it has lost its understanding of 'missionary tongues'. Regarding the shift between Parham's view of tongues, and Seymour's view of tongues, Denzil R. Miller raises the following concern:

There was a definite downside to this theological re-envisioning concerning the nature and purpose of speaking in tongues. With the abandonment the concept of missionary tongues came a marked diminishing of the movement's corporate consciousness of the missionary nature of the

---

[66] *John G. Lake: The Complete Collection of his life teachings*. Roberts Liardon
[67] George Jeffreys: A Ministry of the Miraculous, E.C.W Boulton, p22.

experience of Spirit baptism itself. Over time, Paul's self-edificational view of tongues came to dominate Pentecostal thinking, and Luke's missional view was all but lost, especially in popular teaching and practice.

Miller isn't arguing for Pentecostals to return to the idea that all tongues should be xenoglossia, instead he is arguing that Pentecostals need to understand afresh the missional purpose of tongues. Miller explains:

If tongues is an actual part of the empowerment process, and not just a sign of the same, then tongues becomes a necessary ingredient in missional empowerment.... The believer needs to speak in tongues precisely because tongues is itself part of the empowering work of the Spirit, and therefore a vital key to effective evangelism.

Miller then quotes Scott T. Bottoms in order to explain his argument further:

Luke's goal in emphasizing tongues was not simply to signify the moment a believer is baptized in the Spirit, but as an incarnational sign declaring that the believer's life has been imbued with divine power and purpose. The disciple is now ready for Spirit-empowered ministry and has the access to the empowerment that prayer in tongues brings to an otherwise inconsequential human life.

Miller concludes:

If Bottoms' insights are valid, and I believe that they are, the practice of speaking in tongues is elevated from the (sometimes) narcissistic tongues *as a means of personal blessing construct* held by many Pentecostals and Charismatic Christians today. Tongues are necessary, not simply because they evidence one's reception of the Spirit, but because they are part and parcel of the empowering process itself.

Miller and Bottoms are arguing that both tongues and Spirit baptism must be grounded in the context of Luke's missiology. Tongues are not just intended to be a sign to believers that the Spirit has been received, they are a sign to unbelievers that God is at work. Further, tongues are part of the empowering process for effective mission. In other words, tongues should not just be seen as a means of personal blessing, they should be understood as a means of empowerment for mission.

Whilst not everyone who speaks in tongues can be said to be effective in mission, there are enough testimonies and stories within the history of the Pentecostal and Charismatic movements, and even the present day, to demonstrate that there is (and should be) a connection between tongues and power for mission. In other words, receiving tongues, should equip a believer for effective missional endeavours. Let's look at some real-life examples of tongues and missional effectiveness.

Jackie Pullinger's Story

Jackie Pullinger was called as a missionary to Hong Kong. Yet she struggled with the lack of power in her ministry. After meeting some believers who seemed to be full of life, she was told that she needed to be filled with the Holy Spirit and receive the gift of tongues. Jackie received tongues but she described the experience as a complete anti-climax:

My only emotion that day was embarrassment. … Nothing happened. I tried praying in tongues, but it didn't make me feel close to God. It didn't make me feel anything really. So I stopped. What a disappointment.[68]

Jackie shelved the gift from that point onward. A year later Jackie met an American couple who asked her if she spoke in tongues. She explained how disappointing the experience was. The couple's response took Jackie off-guard. One of them rebuked her:

You are very rude to God. … Whatever made you mistake the gift of the Spirit for the gift of emotion? You're a good evangelical. The Bible says if you speak in tongues you will grow spiritually?; it doesn't say you will *feel* spiritual. You asked for power to preach the gospel. Now get on and use it.[69]

The couple then ask Jackie to commit to praying in

---

[68] *Riding the Third Wave*, Kevin Springer, p236.
[69] Riding, *Springer*, p237.

tongues regularly. She agreed to this and the results on her ministry were world changing. Jackie tells it this way:

By the clock I prayed 15 minutes a day in the language of the Spirit, and still felt nothing as I asked the Spirit to help me intercede for those he wanted to reach. After about six weeks I began to lead people to Jesus without trying. Gangsters fell to their knees sobbing in the streets, women were healed, heroin addicts were miraculously set free. And I knew it all had nothing to do with me.

There is so much to learn from Jackie's story. For me, the key thing is this – can you imagine if she had continued to shelve the gift simply because she never felt anything when she was using it? Further, how many others have stopped using the gift for this reason? Think of all the people who wouldn't have been saved had Jackie not pressed into this gift.

Notice also that she combined praying in tongues with a strong desire for divine appointments. In the past she desired evangelistic success but didn't have any. Now, she expressed her evangelistic desire through praying in tongues and the Spirit was soon able to move through her more powerfully. The point is this, before praying in tongues will release power through us, it must release power in us! It's us that need to be changed. As we spend time praying in the

Spirit, the Holy Spirit is flushing out all the impurities and blockages so that the pure waters of life will flow though us. God doesn't want the lost to be drinking polluted waters. The Spirit must do a refining work in our hearts in order to make us channels of his blessing. The depths of God's Spirit moving through us will be the result of a deep sanctifying work in us.

Imagine what the Lord might do through you or me if we were to give ourselves to the ministry of praying in tongues? Do you not long for people to come to Christ? Do you not long for God's glory to be manifested through healings, deliverances and signs and wonders? Do you not long for people to encounter the risen Jesus? What if all this time that we are waiting for God to move, God is actually waiting for us to move? Pentecost is still being poured out. We just need to turn on the tap. Praying in the Spirit will turn on the tap. As we are faithful in praying in the Spirit, God's presence will flow to us and through us in greater measures.

Jackie's testimony is a contemporary example of the anointing that flowed through tongues in the early Pentecostals. Her story is similar to Smith Wigglesworth's. Wigglesworth was a faithful servant of God, but he did not have a public ministry. He could not express himself well. He was good on a one-to-one basis, but he couldn't speak publicly. Listen to his testimony of what happened when he was filled with the Spirit and began to speak in other tongues.

Smith Wigglesworth's Story

At the time I received the Baptism in the Spirit, a meeting was going on in the large vestry of the All Saints' Church, and I went straight to it. The vicar of the church, Pastor Boddy, had charge and he was speaking. I knew that as yet he had not received the Baptism in the Holy Spirit, and I interrupted him by saying, "Oh, please let me speak, Mr. Boddy; I have just received the Baptism in the Holy Ghost."

The place was full of people. I can't remember what I said, but I know I made all those people extremely dissatisfied and discontented with their position. They said, "We have been rebuking this man because he was so intensely hungry, but he has come in for a few days and has received the Baptism and some of us have been waiting here for months and have not yet received." A great hunger came upon them all. From that day God began to pour out His Spirit until in a very short while fifty had received the Baptism.

The first thing I did was to telegraph to my home saying "I have received the Baptism in the Holy Ghost and have spoken in tongues." On the train to my home town, the Devil began questioning, "Are you going to take this to Bradford?" As regards my feelings at the moment, I had nothing to take, but the just do not live by feelings but by faith. So I shouted out on the railroad coach to everybody's amazement, "Yes, I'm taking it!" A great joy filled me as I made this declaration, but somehow I knew that from that moment it would be a great fight all the time.

When I arrived home … My wife said to me, "So you've been speaking with tongues, have you?" I replied, "Yes." "Well," she said, "It want you to understand that I am as much baptised as you are and I don't speak in tongues." I saw that the contest was beginning right at home. "I have been preaching for twenty years," she continued, "and you have sat beside me on the platform, but on Sunday you will preach yourself, and I'll see what there is in it."

She kept her word. On Sunday she took a seat at the back of the building. We had always sat together on the platform until that day. So the contest had begun right in the church.

There were three steps up to the platform and as I went up those three steps the Lord gave me the scripture in Isaiah 61: 1-3, "The Spirit of the Lord God is upon Me; because the Lord hath anointed Me to preach good tidings unto the meek; He hath sent me to bind up the brokenhearted, to proclaim liberty to the captives, and the opening of the prison to them that are bound." I was no preacher, but hearing the voice of my Lord speaking those words to me, I began. I cannot now remember what I said but my wife was terribly disturbed. The bench on which she sat would seat nine people and she moved about on it until she had sat on every part of it. Then she said in a voice that all around her could hear, "That's not my Smith, Lord, that's not my Smith!"

I was giving out the last hymn when the secretary of the mission stood up and said, "I want what our leader has received." The strange thing was that when he was about to sit down he missed his seat and went right down on the floor. Then my eldest son arose and said he wanted what his father had and he, too, took his seat right down on the floor. In a short while there were eleven people right on the floor of that mission. The strangest thing was that they were all laughing in the Spirit and laughing at one another. The Lord had really turned again the captivity of Zion and the mouth of His children was being filled with laughter according to the word of the Lord in Psalm 126: 1, 2.

This encounter with the Holy Spirit and the ministry of tongues did not just transform Wigglesworth into a powerful preacher. Wigglesworth emerged as a powerful evangelist with the gift of healing. After this encounter with tongues, his ministry was never the same. Roberts Liardon writes:

Under his [Wigglesworth's] ministry, thousands of people came to salvation, committed themselves to a deeper faith in Christ, received the baptism in the Holy Spirit, and were miraculously healed.

Hundreds if not thousands of more stories could be told. And it's not just the heroes of the faith like Wigglesworth, Parham, Lake, Jeffreys, Williams, and Pullinger that share these experiences. Pentecost and its power is available to all who believe and hunger and receive all that God has for them. Wigglesworth, Pullinger and all the other heroes were ordinary believers. They just laid hold of God. Multitudes today are laying hold of God in just the same way. In other words, the church is growing. Western Christianity is no longer the dominant global Christian church. Recent statistics reveal that: "61% of all Christians live in Asia, Africa, and Latin America."[70] Further, the kind of Christianity that is emerging in these parts of the world is a Christianity that shares the core characteristics of the Pentecostal and Charismatic movements. In other words, for the rest of the world, a Christianity that looks like the book of Acts, (complete with Spirit-empowerment, miracles, and persecution) is the 'new normal'. It is not the Pentecostal and Charismatic movement that is the abnormal expression of Christianity, it is the empty shell of the western post-Constantinian church that is the abnormal expression. The church is called to the harvest fields, and to reap the harvest,

---

[70] GlobalChurch: Learning from Majority World Christians (theglobalchurchproject.com)

we need the Spirit's power and tongues of fire. We have a choice. Will we settle for a church life that is a mere shadow of its former self, or will we rekindle the tongues of fire that God has given to his people in order that we will proclaim Christ crucified, buried, risen and ascended with the full power of Pentecost? The choice is ours.

For this reason I remind you to fan into flame the gift of God, which is in you through the laying on of my hands.[7] For the Spirit God gave us does not make us timid, but gives us power, love and self-discipline. (2 Tim. 1:6-7 NIV)

About the Author

John is the pastor of Kairos Church (part of the Apostolic Church UK) and full time English teacher in a local high school. He holds a BD (Hons) in Theology and Pastoral Studies from the Scottish Baptist College, and has been involved in various forms of ministry over the years. He has also authored several books, including his testimony, a 100 Day Devotional, and 'The Lion's Roar: A Prophetic Wake-Up Call'.

Other Books by John Caldwell

Christ, the Cross and the Concrete Jungle

Many communities are ravaged by problems associated with poverty, crime and drug and alcohol abuse. Substantial answers to the urban crisis are all but non-existent. 'Christ, the Cross and the Concrete Jungle' is the story of a young man's deliverance from a lifestyle of desperation and delinquency to a new life of freedom and hope. This books reveals the remarkable journey of transformation and redemption that is made possible through the gospel of Jesus Christ.

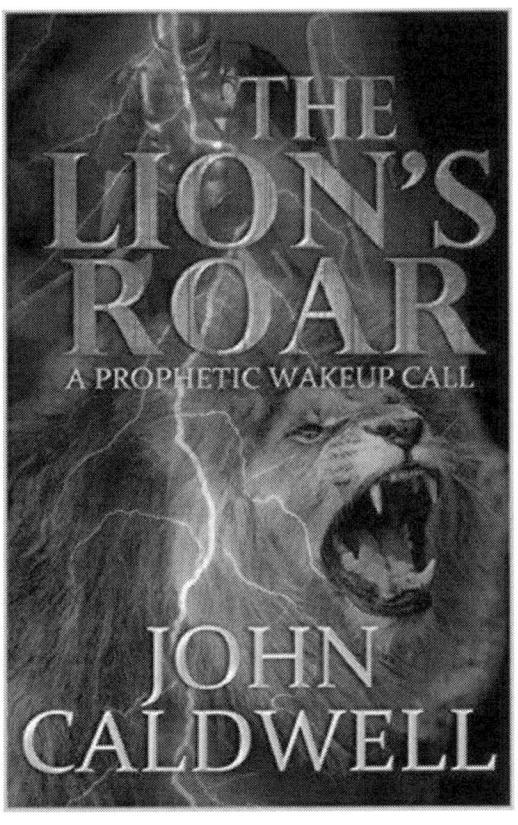

For too long the church has purred like a kitten instead of roaring like a lion. The prophetic voice has been a whimper, when it is supposed to resound like thunder. Think about the church at Pentecost. Pentecost was not a pathetic little shower, it was a raging storm! This is why we need revival – revival is nothing less than God restoring the roar. It's time to hear the Lion's roar, and it's time to awaken the prophetic in order that the church might rise up into the fullness of God's purposes in these final hours.

Vision from the Valleys

'

Vision from the Valleys' takes us not to the Wales of a another era but to a setting into which for a season, at least, God's will was done on earth as in heaven. May all who read be transported not back to a time and place now buried in history but propelled into a contemporary understanding and expression of God's love for the Church and his mission to reach all mankind with the Gospel. This is the heritage of the Apostolic Church, its mantle to help carry and its mission to help fulfil.

Tim Jack (National Leader, Apostolic Church, UK)

When the Fire Fell (Two-Volume Set)

The events surrounding the Azusa Street revival were a catalyst for global mission and a surge of renewal for the worldwide church. Christianity has never been the same. There is a deep recognition amongst many spiritual believers that the contemporary church is in desperate need of a fresh outpouring of the Holy Spirit. These book are a collection of first-hand testimonies, reports, and teachings from the Azusa Street revival and can help us towards that end. It is time to dig the ancient wells. When the Fire Fell is a collection of publications from The Apostolic Faith, a newsletter that helped spread the news of the Azusa Street revival. This collection of papers, now made available in book format, is a great resource for any Christian seeking to build their faith but it is also offered as a resource for students of church history and revival. As you read these accounts of the revival, may your soul be stirred, your faith be fueled, and your prayer be: 'Do it again Lord!"

Printed in Great Britain
by Amazon